TEAMWORK THROUGH FLEXIBLE LEADERSHIP:
A Sharing of Yourself

Rex P. Gatto, Ph.D.

GTA Press

Pittsburgh ◆ 1992

Library of Congress Cataloging-In Publication Data.

Gatto, Rex P.

Teamwork Through Flexible Leadership:
A Sharing of Yourself

Catalog Number: 91-73602

ISBN 0-945997-21-3

Cover design by Mark Symczak

Published by

GTA Press
733 Washington Road, Suite 107
Pittsburgh, PA 15228

Printed in the United States of America

I dedicate this book to my mother,

Paula Cartwright, and father, Angelo Gatto,

who have created the environment of life. Their

values of perseverance, dedication, hope, and

desire and love for learning, and their sense of

regard for life have been an

inspiration for achievement.

Special thanks to Frank Lehner.

TABLE OF CONTENTS

PREFACE

This book provides a unique approach to doing business in today's flexible and changing work environment. Because employees at all levels of the organization need to work productively together, synergism is a must. Employees must combine different areas of expertise and technical knowledge to successfully complete projects on time, within budget, and without wasting resources. By combining talents, employees can better serve their internal and external customers and add to the quality process. "Quality" must become more than just lip service.

An answer to "doing more with less" is through teamwork. Individuals in teams must come together to address business issues through a unity of direction, energy, and commitment, which need to be part of the day-to-day work world. Quality means measuring your success by continually eliminating all deficiencies with products and interacting among people.

By creating teams, you can achieve greater quality, productivity, and worker satisfaction. Obviously, two heads are better than one, and five heads are better than two. But this requires getting people to share ideas, utilizing strengths and developing opportunities to strengthen weaknesses, addressing personal needs, and recognizing and resolving conflict.

Teams—self-directed, corporate, or business sponsored—are viable ways to exchange information and collectively expose individuals' talents as building blocks. The talents of one member of the team can stimulate, excite, and complement another team member's talents. Talents that one person alone might not have developed, or even used, can be exposed because of team dynamics and the building and interactive process.

As we look at "do more with less" and other quality concepts needed to drive organizations, effective use of teams is paramount. We have to find people who can lead the way with competence and confidence—leaders who have followers who believe in them. We must take a proactive approach to making day-to-day decisions, which inspire and help focus followers' energies.

This book discusses various approaches to developing effective teams in a changing business climate. As the title—*Teamwork Through Flexible Leadership: A Sharing of Yourself*—indicates, the team must come together to clearly state objectives, visions, and expected results. This creates a focus of energy and uses everyone's skills and abilities to successfully accomplish and implement business goals while being customer sensitive.

To be effective, teams need to:

- take a call to action;

- create clear goals and direction, know the expected results;

- develop measurable objectives or action strategy to achieve the expected results;

- develop a process to assess and guide or alter the process as needed;

- recognize and applaud achievement; what you reward today is what you will become;

- support through action what the team has agreed on;

- insist on involvement from all members, indicating commitment; and

- support an environment that motivates and encourages teamwork.

Teams will help eliminate wasting time in meetings. People will listen more and take action. Quality will become more than a buzzword. This book will be your guide through the team-building process and into the most beneficial way of doing business in the twenty-first century.

Today and every day should be viewed as a day of jeopardy. That is, what we do today is the reason we will be in business tomorrow. We must place demands on leaders and followers. A new sense of leadership needs to emerge. A leader who leads; not a leader who politically covers all bases and protects executive salaries. We are at a turning point that must be addressed. A new sense of business must replace this worn out entity called *"business as usual."* The challenges of today have never before been seen. It is our new frontier.

THOUGHT PROVOKERS

Complacency leads to the death of creativity. No matter how well a concept works, it should continually be reassessed with regard to creative improvement. Teams challenge and reinvent. They move toward continuous improvement. They make individuals rise to new levels of quality, productivity, and creativity. Success can be our greatest failure if it is not analyzed for improvement.

The more people "know" themselves, the more they will trust themselves and have confidence in their abilities.

> *". . . we must think beyond productivity alone. We must think of organizational health (Bennis) which involves looking at the processes through which problems are solved, not merely at what has been achieved. We must integrate the personal goals of employees with the goals of the organization (McGregor) and we must find those conditions that permit such an integration (Argyris). Going a step further, Blake and Mouton tell us that managers must integrate their concern for production with their concern for people . . ."*

David Lawless
Organizational Behavior

> *"Any business that does not learn how to innovate within the next few years will not be around by the year 2000."*

Peter F. Drucker, 1986
An interview

"A synonym for 'good manager' is 'problem solver.'"

William N. Yeomans, 1985
1000 Things You Never Learned in Business School

"The emphasis is on teamwork and results, and the objectives derived from the goals of the business."

Peter F. Drucker, 1954
Practice of Management

"Leadership is also a transaction, a transaction between leaders and followers. . . . The management of meaning, mastery of communication, is inseparable from effective leadership."

Warren Bennis, Burt Nanus, 1985
Leaders: The Strategy for Taking Charge

"The art of leadership: liberating people to do what is required of them in the most effective and humane way possible."

Max DePree, 1989
Leadership Is an Art

1

LEADERSHIP—A CHANGING TRADITION

The concept of leadership as we know it is a relatively new science. Prior to the twentieth century, leaders were born into a position of leadership (kings and queens), or they were the most powerful warrior, courageous knight, or famous general. In modern day we have leaders such as Lee Iacocca, Martin Luther King, Jr., Lech Walesa, Mother Theresa—all with various backgrounds and values. However, there are dimensions that seem to transcend background.

Today's leaders take advantage and act in the opportunity that is given to them. They have the courage to go beyond what people think, and risk who and what they are for the opportunity to demonstrate their desire and ability to give of themselves. These leaders are motivated by an inner drive to fulfill themselves through the expression and process of inspiring others to follow. Yet, history teaches that leaders like Adolph Hitler and Reverend Jim Jones are toxic and destructive, while Ghandi and Mother Theresa lead with love and compassion.

Let's examine the dimensions from and upon which leaders draw their ability to challenge themselves to be willing to lead.

1. Leaders have the **knowledge** to establish a strategy and method or basis for action. They have the inner strength and mental resources or demonstrate the knowledge needed to establish their plan. They surround themselves with the right advisors who believe in what they say.

2. Leaders have the **competence** to lead. The competence varies in many ways among leaders, but they use what is right for that time in an environment that supports their style of leadership and people will follow.

3. Leaders are **flexible** to changing business needs and personal needs of their followers. They do whatever it takes to accomplish the job, inspire people to change or alter their course when needed, and adapt to become successful. Rigidity is the downfall of many leaders. They are not flexible. As powerful as Hitler was, his inflexibility crumbled his empire. Flexibility is what built many corporations—the risk to follow leaders like Thomas Edison and George Westinghouse.

4. Leaders have the ability to **listen** and understand others' opinions and ideas. This gives the leader the ability to bridge and clarify ideas, to build upon team ideas and incorporate and synthesize the ideas of their advisors.

5. Leaders also have the ability to **convey** and express their ideas in such a way that followers understand and emotionally buy in to the ideas to implement and act upon the idea. They are charismatic.

6. Leaders create **trust**—"I say it and I follow through." They express and learn from mistakes, yet encourage success through openness, sharing of power, gaining consensus, showing support, recognizing diligent work. They show trust by letting the followers challenge themselves.

7. Leaders have the **confidence** to realize that failure is a reason to continue rather than end. They have the inner fortitude to inspire because of values and belief in what is right. They show confidence in plans to succeed rather than avoiding failure.

8. Leaders **take action**. They assess risks, challenging inner talents of others to make a call to action. They establish the purpose of this action, the expected results, and a realistic time frame to hold people accountable to act and achieve. They allow the people who have their hands on the action to make decisions.

9. Leaders know the **ability of followers**: who they are and what they value. They know what the followers are willing to fight for and what they are capable of doing. They know where one follower's performance and ability might support another follower's performance and ability.

10. Leaders know what they are **capable** of doing. They have the inner strength to expose themselves as leaders. They're not afraid of criticism or the "stones people throw." Churchill inspired a nation to fight, Martin Luther King led a people to great heights; both had an inner strength and knew the leadership ability they possessed.

Leadership is a simple concept: It is the process to establish a direction, support this with action, and be willing to inspire people on all levels to achieve the vision. Leadership is sharing your business knowledge, wisdom, and humaneness.

These dimensions of leadership encourage the integrity and nature of what leaders do to lead successfully. Yet the gesture, tone, stature, eye contact, sincerity, and touch can't be taught. Where do the characteristics begin to develop? They come from our grandparents who give us history; our parents who guide and slowly relinquish to us our own sense of empowerment; the values and perspectives of friends and teachers; and from the pain and joys of life. These characteristics come from inner strength—a sharing of yourself.

"Leaders are people who do the right thing; managers are people who do things right. Both roles are crucial, but they differ profoundly. I often observe people in top positions doing wrong things well."

Warren Bennis, 1989
Why Leaders Can't Lead

Effective leaders use various leadership styles— by supporting people's abilities and skills and determining the appropriate leadership style to use.

Effective leaders trust themselves to act in unpredictable situations and help the workforce get back to doing essential aspects of business. They develop themselves while leading and developing others to do the right things. Effective leaders know when to act and when to listen and follow.

Successful leaders apply their abilities to the opportunity, not to creating opportunities for personal power or gain.

L eaders develop through ability, desire, and opportunity.

E ffectively develop followers.

A ddress issues proactively.

D evelop their potential by modeling and making decisions.

E arn the respect of their followers.

R esponsible to act.

S ingle out and clearly define expectations.

H ave the desire and trust to lead in unpredictable circumstances.

I dentify the right questions and actions.

P rovide open, honest, trusting, and respectful communication.

There is no one way to lead effectively; however, leaders must take into consideration:

- Their abilities and skills as a leader.
- The level of maturity, comprehension, and ability of the employees.
- What is appropriate in a given circumstance, changing situation, or environment.
- Business or corporate expectations versus personal needs.
- Personal desire to achieve and act decisively on a given opportunity.

LEADERSHIP PERFORMANCE MODEL

The Leadership Performance Model is a general guide to help you access how you learn and process concepts of leadership. You will also be able to better identify your leadership process. There should be follow-up application utilizing your leadership strengths and continual reassessment of your performance as a leader with regard to what you might need to become an "effective leader."

LEADERSHIP PERFORMANCE MODEL

AWARENESS

Knowledge; acquisition of information.
Understanding of leadership and followership.
Choosing the most effective style of leadership.
Perceiving information.
Interpreting information.
Giving information meaning.

RE-EVALUATE

Questioning, challenging, or reinforcing awareness of leadership and followership through application and feedback.

Redefining which style of leadership was appropriate.

How will you apply what you learned to enhance your leadership and followership skills?

APPLICATION

Interactively using your awareness of leadership ([Say = Do] = trust)

Clearly communicating the big picture/ specifics and individual responsibility.

Leadership style.

Meetings: listen and explain.

Write reports and make presentations.

Acquiring the appropriate results.

FEEDBACK

Evaluating leadership and followership effectiveness.
Feedback process; share ideas of support and corrective action.
Determine what was appropriate.
Introspection/Self-assessment.
Performance appraisal/Feedback from others.
What changes would you make?

LEADERSHIP

Definition: **A process** by which leaders guide and develop themselves and others by communicating direction, taking appropriate action, building trust, and achieving goals, given: the leader's abilities and skills, the abilities and skills of the followers, within a changing environment.

Leadership skills are what you and others observe and perceive. Our leadership abilities are within us and are a constant and stable factor. However, our level of leadership skills varies because of opportunity, stress, frustration, employee abilities, your abilities and desires, and time limitation. Stress and/or anxiety might lessen our skills as an effective leader. Be cognizant of your level of leadership skills and when and how it may vary.

FOUR STYLES OF LEADERSHIP

No one style of leadership is best. The most appropriate style of leadership depends on the situation, relationship, and the abilities of the leader and follower(s). Therefore, effective leaders need to be flexible. Think of leadership as a tight-loose relationship—setting "tight" parameters, policies, procedures, responsibilities; then turning the followers "loose" to accomplish their respective duties.

Keep in mind that each style of leadership is a strong indicator of how the team works together. Each style is a statement of trust and a level of shared energy. This is the beginning of a partnering: a realization of giving and asking for; in a work relationship, a bonding that causes us to realize a level of accomplishment.

Direct Style

This is an authoritarian or directing leadership style, high in control with a priority toward results. This style of leader supervises very closely the decision-making process. The rapport between the leader and follower is task oriented and geared toward getting the job done. This style is appropriate for new followers or followers who might not have a high level of comprehension or competence, desire, and/or ability, given the job to be accomplished. The leader must initiate, organize, and direct to accomplish the task. Also, if there is not sufficient time to have high interaction, then this style might be appropriate. The danger many leaders fall into is, "I can do it better than the follower." Therefore, the leader does the job. When the leader does the job, the leader, in essence, becomes a follower. This is not right or wrong, but is it appropriate?

Generally this style does not develop followers because it does not allow them to learn how to accomplish the task on their own. In addition, followers typically do not receive due recognition for the completed job. The leader using this style should continually reassess the follower's abilities. When the follower has the expertise to achieve and there is sufficient time, another style of leadership might be appropriate.

Share/Consult Style

This style of leadership expands upon the direct style, with a higher degree of interaction between the leader and follower. There is now an exchange of ideas concerning what needs to be accomplished. The leader can be task oriented, as well as people oriented, and can act as an advisor. The leader interacts, coaches, motivates, and advises the follower to share in the process of achieving.

This style is appropriate when there is sufficient time to interact with and develop followers' abilities. However, the leader basically controls, because the follower might need to develop more confidence and/or competence. This style begins with the interactive process of sharing ideas with the follower(s) about the task. The followers might have expectations that require acting on what was shared; clearly set ground rules help ensure expected results. The leader needs to clarify the purpose and importance for sharing information and possible outcomes. Leaders have to be aware not to dominate the sharing process. They have to listen to and integrate what the follower says and clarify agreement or resolve conflict.

Participative Style

This style of leadership builds upon the share/consult style and might develop a trusting relationship between the leader and follower. The leader displays faith in the follower's abilities to complete job responsibilities and builds an interactive relationship in discussing what is to be accomplished. Because today's employees are more sophisticated and educated, it is critical that leaders overshare information that is not proprietary. Today more than ever it is critical to inform employees to build trust. Example— Bill Jones, Executive Vice President of Koppers Engineering, suggests to provide a broad guide for the employees to let them set objectives. This lets the employees own the objectives. He suggests leaders listen and collect feedback. If leaders trust employees and employees trust leaders, then we will have open communication. Bill further suggests that leaders get to know employees.

This leadership style is high in interpersonal and low in task orientation and further builds an interactive rapport. The leader listens, accepts, and cooperates with the follower and encourages participation in the decision-making process. This style is appropriate when there needs to be a high degree of interaction and synergism in accomplishing the task and the employee shows a degree of work-related competence.

Many authors and experts view the participative style as a very necessary and effective approach to leadership. "The management of meaning, mastery of communication, is inseparable from effective leadership." ("LEADERS" Bennis and Nanus, 1985, p. 33.) This is an effective style because it encourages leaders and competent followers to develop their interactive skills and lets followers emerge as leaders by completing the job with less control on the part of the leader. It also opens lines of communication so the follower(s) can express their viewpoints and be used as a resource.

It builds upon the share/consult style by permitting followers to have input accepted and utilizes their job-related competence. It is important that the leader inform follower(s) about decisions; not being informed could hinder the level of participation. This participative style helps the leader share and collect information, as well as lets the follower begin to become involved in making decisions. The leader must be an effective listener and willing to initiate action based on the participative process.

Empower/Delegate Style

This style is derived from the participative style; it encourages the follower to initiate action. This style is appropriate when the follower demonstrates a high degree of competence and confidence. The follower should need little encouragement to accomplish job responsibilities. There is a lower degree of interaction and control by the leader because now the follower emerges as a leader.

The leader and follower should develop an effective working rapport and establish mutual trust. The leader must trust that the job will be successfully accomplished, yet from a distance measure the progress. However, the follower should be permitted to make necessary decisions to complete the job. This lets the follower use and develop skills as a leader.

To empower means that the follower is willing to accept the responsibility of doing the job and has the freedom to make decisions. The leader maintains positional authority by authorizing the follower and further confides in the follower. Often leaders think of delegation as empowerment, letting the followers do the "dirty work," yet keeping the decision-making power. This is not empowerment; it is simple task assignment. Furthermore, to empower means that the follower has a sense of purpose, knows what is to be accomplished, values what he/she is doing, and has the freedom to make choices to accomplish the job or task. The leader holds the empowered follower accountable, but turns the person loose to accomplish. The leader still has a responsibility to see that the job is accomplished, which might translate to: on time, within budget, and organizationally implemented. This leadership style can be a developmental process for the follower *and* the leader. This can be the test for a leadership succession plan in developing future leaders.

SUMMARY

To lead effectively, the leader must choose a style of leadership that best fits his/her abilities in leading, the abilities of the followers, and the changing work environment. It is essential that leaders demonstrate qualities of a clear communicator, trust, competence, and confidence in establishing a business direction. The *Leadership/Followership Model* which follows— starting with the direct style (high in control)—moves toward empowerment (developing leadership and followership). Study the *Leadership/Followership Model* and examine the inverse relationship in control and empowerment (tight-loose relationship) and the developmental leadership and followership process.

LEADERSHIP/FOLLOWERSHIP MODEL

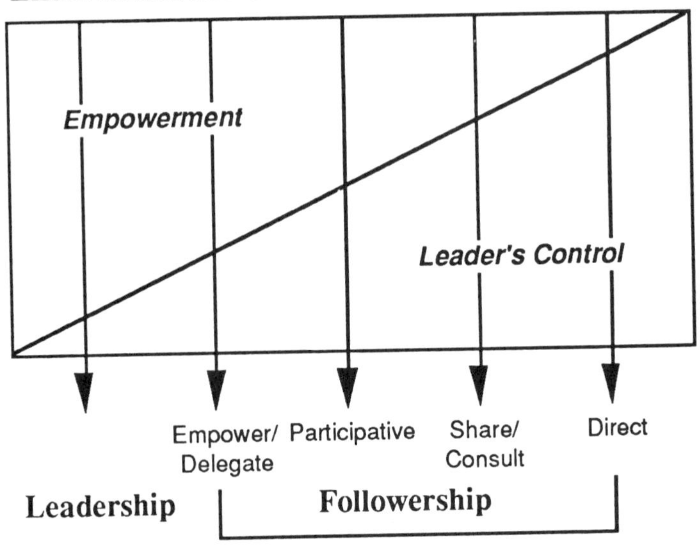

There are two basic principles that give insight into modern concepts of leadership: the scientific management by Fredrick Taylor (1911) and the Hawthorne Study (1930). The premise for scientific management is that people need to be controlled—discover the best way to do a particular job, divide a job into its simplest components, and establish a piece rate incentive (you get paid for what you have done). With the Hawthorne Effect at Western Electric in the 1920-30s, researchers conducted a study on lighting, work breaks, and other conditions in the workplace. The results were that, because someone showed an interest or concern in the employees, productivity improved. The scientific management principle is high in control and results oriented; the Hawthorne Effect is geared toward interest or involvement with the employees. These two principles will be further explained in Chapter 7. This is a brief overview of how we view a leader—control over the employee or involvement with the employee.

This is a delicate balancing act between controlling, dictating/directing (control), sharing/consulting, participating (people), and empowering/delegating. A leader needs to use all four styles appropriately.

Examine the Leadership Styles Grid on the next page. Think of where you would place yourself as a follower, then as a leader with various levels of employees.

LEADERSHIP STYLES GRID

Leader's Control with Employees: Task Oriented (TO)—
Leader shows concern for, or focuses on, getting work done or
accomplishing tasks; directs the process.

**Leader's Involvement with Employees: People Oriented
(PO)—**Leader shows concern for, or focuses on, people's needs
and feelings and begins to build relationships with people; gives
the competent follower freedom.

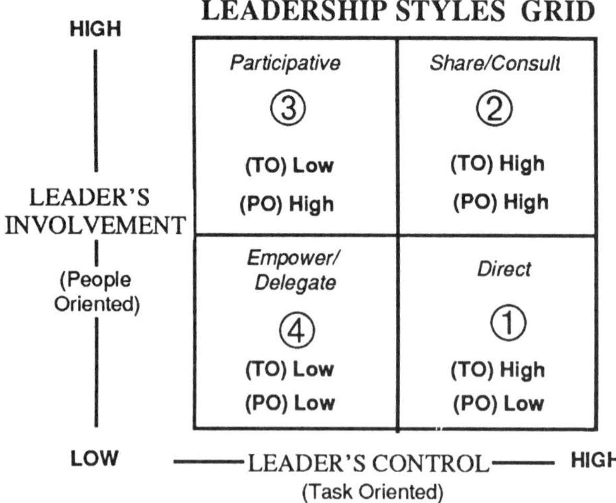

Examine each quadrant to note if you are:

① High task oriented/low people oriented
② High task oriented/high people oriented
③ Low task oriented/high people oriented
④ Low task oriented/low people oriented

Effective leaders choose an appropriate leadership
style/orientation based on their abilities, the followers'
abilities, and the particular demands in the situation,
circumstance, or work environment.

To be an effective leader means that you would ask the right question before answering, listen, understand the people and task needs, and appropriately act. These leadership concepts are further explored through leadership theories.

LEADERSHIP

In this section, we will examine theories of leadership. These theories are a foundation to understanding organizational culture via the leader's role. To explain this, picture an umbrella. At the top is the point of the organization, the CEO/Chairman. As the umbrella opens, the layers of leaders are exposed. The more layers of management, the more difficult it is to have clear communication. The more layers of management the more interpretations of policies, procedures, rules, and regulations.

The new philosophy is to cut layers of management and make the organization more flexible. Each leader, regardless of level, is held accountable for action. Leaders can be understood and analyzed through the Leadership Styles Grid and the following leadership theories.

TRANSACTIONAL LEADER *(Bass)*

1. Recognizes what followers want to get from the work and tries to see that they get it.

2. Exchanges rewards, and promises of reward, for effort expended by followers.

3. Responds to followers' immediate self-interests based on their work performance. Is generally liked—rarely admired.

4. Leads during a period of calm and inactivity. Is soon forgotten after leadership ceases.

5. Deals with efficiency; interested in what will work; sets goals and explains how to achieve them.

TRANSFORMATION LEADER *(Bass)*

1. Motivates followers to do more than they are expected to do; pushes them beyond their original levels of confidence.

2. Raises followers' level of awareness about the importance of designated outcomes and ways of reaching them.

3. Gets followers to transcend self-interests for the sake of the organization. Is charismatic; followers develop intense feelings about such leaders, and want to follow them; have trust and confidence in them.

4. Often emerges in times of stress. Influences others and is often remembered.

5. Deals with developing ideas; develops followers to be responsible for their own actions.

TRADITIONAL LEADERSHIP STYLES

Autocratic—Characteristics of Theory X (McGregor)

Management is responsible for organizing the elements of production in the interest of economic/educational ends.

People *must be directed,* motivated, and controlled, and their behavior must be modified to fit the needs of the organization.

People are normally passive; management motivates through outside incentives.

People are indolent (lazy), lack ambition, like to be led, are indifferent to organizational needs, self-centered, and resistant to change.

Democratic—Characteristics of Theory Y (McGregor)

Management is responsible for organizing the elements of production in the interest of economic/educational ends.

Management is responsible for making it possible for *people to develop for themselves* the motivation, capacity to assume responsibility, and desire to direct behavior toward organizational goals.

People *are not normally passive,* but become so through experiences in organizations.

Management has to arrange organizational conditions and methods of operations so that people can achieve their own goals by directing their own efforts toward organizational objectives.

Characteristics of Theory Z (Ouchi)

Recognizes that management style must adjust to the needs of the organization at whatever state of evolution it has reached.

Adapts the style to the organization depending on the level of evolution the organization has achieved.

Is suspect of absolutes.

Realizes that objective awareness of the demands of the unique group and organization, even of the unique individual, is the ideal (which is rarely reached). Recognizes and works toward the ideal.

LEADERSHIP PATTERNS *(Argyris)*

Pattern A Hard

Behavior manifested in Theory X Assumptions; strong leadership, tight control, close supervision; watch each step of the supervised.

Pattern A Soft

Tight control, disguised by buying, persuading, or winning over people to obtain compliance and acceptance of direction from supervisor.

Pattern B

Behavior manifested in Theory Y Assumptions; commitment to an identification with worthwhile objectives in the work context; building of mutual trust and respect in an interpersonal context; meaningful satisfaction achieved by the individual within the context of accomplishment of important work within the organization.

DETERMINANTS OF LEADERSHIP PATTERNS

Supervisory style is selected and determined by three forces:

1. Within the Supervisor

    A. Own value system
    B. Confidence in subordinates
    C. Leadership inclinations
    D. Security in uncertain situations

2. Within the Supervisory Environment (which has many variable influences)

3. Within Others (subordinates/management)

LEADERSHIP DEVELOPMENT *(Argyris)*

Becoming an effective leader is no easy task. It is an ongoing, ever-changing process that fluctuates with various people, situations, and environments. By constantly monitoring your style and making adjustments, you'll achieve the greatest success and satisfaction, as will those who follow your lead.

Following are some guidelines to help you improve, maintain, and enhance your leadership style.

From	**To**
1. Passive; having to be stimulated, motivated, and disciplined.	Active states of being self-reliant, self-initiated, and self-determined.
2. Dependent or lacking confidence.	Relative independence, to interdependence (internalization of a set of values that become base for behavior).
3. Capable of behaving in a few ways.	Flexible, capable of behaving in many different ways.
4. Unpredictable interests of short duration.	Deeper and varied interests.

5. Short-sighted perspectives.	Much larger time perspective of events; behavior is affected by past events and future hopes.
6. Subordinate position.	Aspire to occupy an equal and/or superordinate position in reference to peers.
7. Lack of self-awareness.	Awareness of and control over oneself.

These guidelines help us to understand the type of people who lead. As leaders, we may now better understand ourselves. As followers, we may better understand those we follow through enjoyment or resistance.

Don't feel that because you have read examples of styles and theories about leadership you know the *concept*. The concept of leadership is ever evolving and is judged differently each decade by a changing people. It is far better to question the concept of leadership than to say you know it.

2

TO MANAGE OR NOT TO MANAGE?

Every author and lecturer has an opinion on the proper methods of managing employees. Although there is a multitude of management techniques in practice, the task and interpersonal orientation with employees is the most common.

The traditional concept of superior (supervisor or manager)-subordinate (employee) has almost disappeared with the advent of participative management. Employees realize that they are an integral part of an organization and want their "fair share." As employees proceed through a career, they acquire more self-esteem as they gain more authority, which builds through promotion and business contacts. This base of authority develops into power (superior-subordinate) over new or lower-ranking employees.

The main ingredient for success within a person is self-esteem: competence and confidence in oneself.

How does a manager, while pushing for job efficiency (task) and increased productivity, build self-esteem and develop potential in each employee (interpersonal)? This is done by building and developing employees' confidence to reach potential (technical and people orientation). Today's manager should be a leader who is in search of the meaning of leadership. A leader should define leadership qualities and establish rapport with all employees, understanding the environment in which the employees work. A manager who is a leader is continually adapting to meet employees' work demands and is continually adapting to meet employee needs. By following this conceptual process, a manager is managing by adaptation. Researchers have found that employees' job efficiency (daily productivity) averages 40 to 60 percent. This seems to be an accepted norm, and the status quo remains. However, to improve the status quo, managers can guide, listen to, and nurture employees.

When leaders define and clearly discuss job expectations for themselves and others, job productivity for the business team increases.

> *"Up to a third of the work in U.S.*
> *companies is work that is being done*
> *again because of quality deficiencies."*

> J. Juran, 1989

Managers need to realize that it is necessary to communicate, not from the perspective of a managerial level, but from an employee level. Employees cannot be held accountable for development if they do not have all the necessary information concerning organizational, internal and external, and *customers'* needs.

Management, by adapting to a task- and people-oriented style, will build a working rapport of trust and respect between the employee and manager. "Management by Adaptation" encourages the manager and employee to accept that everyone does not have to conform to a specific mode of operation. There is no one way to manage or to supervise employees. Rather, an individual mode of operation that conforms with general policy should be mutually discussed among all employees and the supervisor/manager, and then implemented. An outline of the basic tenets of the technique of "Management by Adaptation" follows.

MANAGEMENT BY ADAPTATION (MBA)

Managers must be aware of their own uniqueness, what they do best, their sense of genius, and, at the same time, understand the uniqueness of others. Employees are individuals with various strengths who will implement different strategies for completing a job. Here are keys to an effective leadership style.

1. Successfully communicate all necessary information to employees on an equal basis.

2. Clearly define the job role of each employee.

3. Mutually establish expected results and methods of action to achieve those results with employees.

4. Reassess expected results and methods of action with each employee.

5. Utilize the right person for the specific job function.

6. Have employees perform necessary tasks and give them credit for their achievements.

7. Allow employees to meet changing business needs.

8. Keep employees informed/updated.

9. Reassess daily business needs in relation to human resources available.

10. Give employees the freedom to meet job expectations via their individual mode of working.

11. Build an open, trusting, respectful, and honest rapport with all employees.

12. Recognize employees when they deserve it.

These twelve points are keys that can open doors to a successful manager-employee relationship. They build a strong foundation toward success/achievement.

"Communication" is one of the most widely used words in the business world today. As often as the word communication is used, it still has an ambivalent meaning that changes depending upon who uses the word.

Managers and employees must build a communication rapport to complete their jobs and fulfill corporate and customer needs effectively. There should be trust in sharing customer and business strategies, however significant or minor. Too often employees are tentative to have honest communication because they think it will somehow impact their evaluation. This type of manager-employee rapport is typical of the superior-subordinate relationship, which is not very constructive.

When the employee and leader continually share ideas through a task and interpersonal rapport, openness will develop. If a collaborative relationship is established, rather than a superior-subordinate relationship, communication skills will be greatly enhanced and the twelve keys previously mentioned will begin to be implemented. Open communication is the glue that holds these twelve keys together.

The key to successful communication is the clear understanding of corporate, employee, management, and customer needs, which can be translated into measurable actions. In order to successfully perform, all of the people involved must have their needs clearly understood, thereby having a chance to fulfill expectations. Once these needs are clearly understood, then the business team can develop its focus and follow-up. This communication is measurable and ties into the concept of quality: ask the right question; take the right action; and do it the first time.

If the responsibilities of the business world are delineated by communication, active and passive communication can be analyzed. Active communication is face-to-face, written, or via phone interaction. Inactive (passive) communication is the interpretation and explanation of expected results and methods of action by a third party. Examples are: service or sales employees interacting with a customer (active communication) on behalf of management (inactive communication); a supervisor telling employees a top management decision (inactive); or a support staff explaining (active) a supervisor's expected results (inactive) to other support staff.

To have clear communication, all parties must be informed and know that their expectations can be met. Clear communication is dependent upon a cycle of communication. The service/sales and support staff are the pivot between customer and management. As long as the front-line staff people are able to communicate internal and external customer needs to management, and management listens and responds, communication will result in higher productivity. This is, however, easy to state and difficult to implement.

There are two basic ways in which we communicate in an organization: action and words. Action includes do what I say, modeling, demonstrating, implementing, acting, and nonverbal body language, eye contact, facial expression. Both written and verbal (face-to-face, via the phone) communication create a message. Verbal communication should exhibit sincerity and honesty through tone, expression, and volume. The written and verbal word impart concepts of life and reality. Most people today want clear, concise concepts—bulleted points—as a general rule of thumb for effective communication.

The concept of layers of communication was discussed in Chapter 1. The idea of active and inactive communication plays an important part in understanding why layers of management can deter organizational productivity. The original statement and subsequent interpretations might not create clear communication throughout the organization. Employees may work hard doing the wrong thing because of improper communication. Example: Change is not communicated and productivity suffers.

Verbal communication is not the most effective way to communicate. When you listen to someone speak, you have to listen at the speaker's rate of delivery. You can't review what is said word for word. A written statement is received at the reader's rate—word for word—which reinforces the communication and can easily be reviewed.

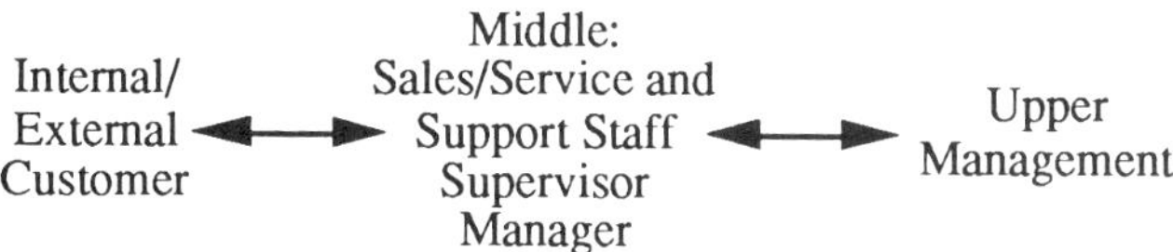

The cycle of corporate communication can become disrupted by poor interpretation by supervisor/manager and service/sales/support staff; lack of management action; customers with unrealistic demands that management attempts to meet; lack of support for service and/or sales employees; or unclear or unexpected results.

If the first step of communication is not achieved by the manager and employee, it is unlikely that there will be significant development in any other area between them and the 12 points of MBA will be lost. Each will remain in a fixed state, letting each other know just enough information to get the job done at a minimal level of efficiency and productivity. Good communication liberates us to do our jobs better. Clear corporate communication allows us to respond to the demands placed on us and to carry out our responsibilities. Through clear communication the MBA technique will reach its pinnacle. This also means that leaders can use communication to free the people reporting to them.

To liberate people, communication must be based on logic, compassion, and sound reasoning.

Max DePree, 1989, p. 107

No reason justifies a lack of employee potential development in a job position. Philosophically, as an employee advances through the corporation, many doors are opened and closed. The key that opens the most doors is communication. What one knows, and how one says it, is directly proportionate to success. It is what you say, along with how you say it, that gets results. Leaders should manage by honestly communicating with themselves, and then realize their needs and the needs of the employees.

Only after there is an understanding, through clear communication, can the remaining 11 concepts of **MBA** be achieved by logically working through the process of guiding and developing employees through their task- and people-oriented job responsibilities.

One of the first concepts established by Henry Ford was a specific job role for each employee. This is still an important rule for leaders to follow today. It is imperative that employees clearly understand the totality of their jobs. Many times leaders assume or expect employees to act in a certain manner to complete a job without clearly defining the expected results. Employee assumptions, without guidance, can lead to poor morale and employee turnover; employees often vote with their feet. Employees need to know specifically what is expected and be given the opportunity to complete these expectations in methods consistent with their style of working, provided the methods meet corporate policy. It is impossible to meet anyone else's expectations unless those expectations become incorporated or adapted into the individual's expectations. By letting employees have the freedom and autonomy to complete the job expectations in a method they are comfortable with, job productivity can be enhanced.

As employees begin to create a methodology to fulfill the requirements of their jobs, the leader should help them establish how they will fulfill the expected results of that job's responsibilities (and complete and support quarterly and yearly action plans). Both the leader and employee should be comfortable with the action plan to accomplish expected job results. Effective communication is necessary to mutually establish the concepts needed to fulfill expected job responsibilities and methods of action. What is praised today through performance appraisal will become the standard of the future. This is a strong message throughout the organization.

To fulfill customer, executive, individual, and job expectations, employees should reassess daily accomplishments. Successful daily task performance leads to successful quarterly results. Yet, too often the focus on expected results is emphasized annually. The problem with yearly examination of expected results is that improper methods of action might be established and not easily changed. What is the message this sends throughout the organization? Leaders should guide employees and collect feedback daily, weekly, and/or monthly to ensure that the methods of action are "properly" fulfilling the expected results. This is a clear message of accountability that is communicated. The MBA technique supports continual, frequent updates.

Brief meetings with employees allow continual reassessment of actions and assessment of expected results, which will ensure realistic expectations. Leaders and employees should prepare by setting priorities that need to be accomplished in the meeting. By mutually establishing job expectations and ways to accomplish those expectations, the employee and leader will have better insight into the utilization of the employee's potential.

Meetings can then be brief, informative, and successful. In addition, the ability to lead group meetings and discussions on an improvised basis is as important as the prepared detailed meeting. Even if the employees perform the same labor-intensive job expectations, regular meetings will let them feel involved and a part of the corporation by sharing ideas.

When employees begin to meet individual and corporate expectations, they become part of a business team. A leader who guides employees to meet corporate expectations can begin to utilize a team of employees by having them complement each other's job performances. Leaders who recognize employees for their accomplishments give these employees the impetus to continue. A leader who takes the time to recognize and identify styles of operation will be successful in utilizing employees' potential toward corporate benefit.

The basis for accomplishing team interaction is dependent upon the leader's qualities. Successful leadership is based on effective communication, consistent or stable actions and proactions, and the commitment to follow through. The 12 keys of MBA can be a benchmark for building leader-follower rapport and a business focus. If the leader exhibits a consistent style of managing and incorporates employees' freedom to fulfill their job roles in their own styles, productivity may very well be enhanced. Management should provide the focus of corporate concepts, and leaders should guide employees to fulfill corporate concepts and meet customer/client needs.

Leadership skills are not learned through acquired information; rather, they are learned through application of acquired information that eventually develops individual abilities. Techniques espoused by an author or lecturer are useless unless applied to enhance individual productivity. Management has a responsibility to fulfill executive expectations with the guidance and development of themselves and all employees. Improved employee morale and increased productivity must be achieved by allowing corporate expectations to be accomplished through each employee's contribution.

Turning employees loose with clarity of direction without continuous intervention is important. But is this a reality in today's business world? What pressures or mind set do you go to work with? Are you: an employee, mother, father, friend or expert, angry, a victim, a loser, a power seeker, a political promotion seeker? Analyze your mind set or personal priorities. Assess your hidden agenda when you are at work. How can you implement the MBA technique when outside pressures preclude your ability to even do what you believe should be accomplished?

ESTABLISHING PERSONAL PRIORITIES

On a scale of 1 to 10, rank these pressures that create anxiety.

1	indicates the greatest pressure
10	indicates the least pressure creating anxiety

_______   recognition/promotion

_______   trying to feel good about myself/self-esteem

_______   time/meeting fixed deadlines

_______   creative challenges of the job

_______   job evaluation by my supervisor/manager

_______   corporate demands/wants

_______   money and financial security

_______   maintaining job productivity/quality

_______   developing a business team approach

_______   boss's wants

_______   ____________________________________

(If needed, list your own pressure-creating anxiety and drop one from the list above.)

Do these pressures preclude you from communicating more effectively—taking the action you believe should be taken?

Tie these pressures to the Maslow Motivational or Needs Model. This self-assessment may very well help you understand why you might take action contrary to your beliefs or values in the workplace.

MASLOW'S HIERARCHY OF NEEDS

Each level must be fulfilled or satisfied before you can continue to the next level. This is a process by which you can fulfill yourself through developing potential.

Physiological Needs	Life-sustaining needs; the most basic and powerful human needs (e.g., food, shelter, love, sleep). Do you go to work concerned about family needs, mortgage/college payments, monthly bills, etc.?
	Work Examples: Paycheck, work breaks, equipment, work conditions, deadlines.
Safety/Self-preservation	You are free from anxiety and insecurity because of the neighborhood, workplace, family, etc. Do you work in a job that is hazardous, physically or emotionally (i.e., a high risk-exposure position)?
	Work Examples: Job security, work standards, seniority, evaluation.

Belonging	Need for love; you are accepted and given affection in relationships. Do you have marital problems, trouble in a relationship with someone, or a sense of being all alone?
	Work Examples: Teamwork, social group, friendly manager.
Self-esteem	Recognition of self; having a feeling of worth. Do you have self-doubt, question yourself even when a decision has been made (i.e., worry about it)?
	Work Examples: promotion, praise, special benefits, earned recognition, appreciation.
Self-actualization	You desire to become your potential—this is a continuum. Are you challenged, and do you feel you have or are accomplishing tasks by using your talents?
	Work Examples: Creativity, self-realization, challenges of work, achievement, advancement.

These inner thoughts might be why you avoid any of the MBA points (assess and reflect). Are you reaching what you are capable of achieving? Realize that work is only a part of how you demonstrate your talent. I know a well-respected hospital administrator, who, when asked, says he is a musician because he has played trumpet since he was a child. What is he? The point of this brief exercise is for you to ask yourself questions, be reflective, and go beyond superficial thoughts of business.

HIERARCHY OF NEEDS

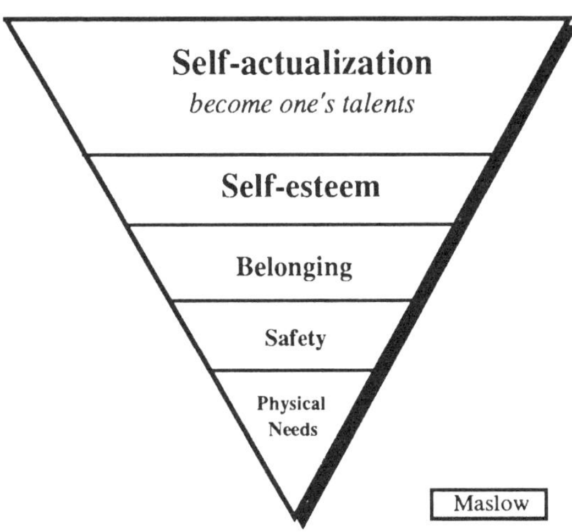

This model is inverted from the traditional presentation. This emphasizes the building process of growth toward developmental self-actualization.

STRATEGIES

To help others attain their levels of need and potential, you must first address your barriers and roadblocks. On the following page, list the top three pressures from your inventory and apply them to Maslow's Hierarchy. Write the level in which you think you are working, then write a strategy of how to overcome your greatest pressures.

In which level are you generally working?

Pressures	**Maslow's Hierarchy Corresponding Level**

examples:

1. <u>Boss wants</u>   1. <u>Safety, belonging</u>

2. Creative Challenges
   <u>of Job</u>   2. <u>Self-actualization</u>

3. _______________   3. _______________

Strategies for addressing your greatest pressures:

____

____

____

____

____

____

____

____

____

____

____

COMPARING YOU AND OTHERS

Compare your pressures with those you perceive as others' pressures and wants. List what you see as common strengths, weaknesses, acceptances, and rejections between you, other employees, and your boss. There are no right or wrong answers. Each characteristic could change from a strength to weakness depending on with whom you are working.

Example: Talkative person in some situations is a strength that is accepted; other situations rejected. Some situations could be considered a weakness. Be reflective and think about yourself in the workplace.

CORPORATE CULTURE DIAGRAM

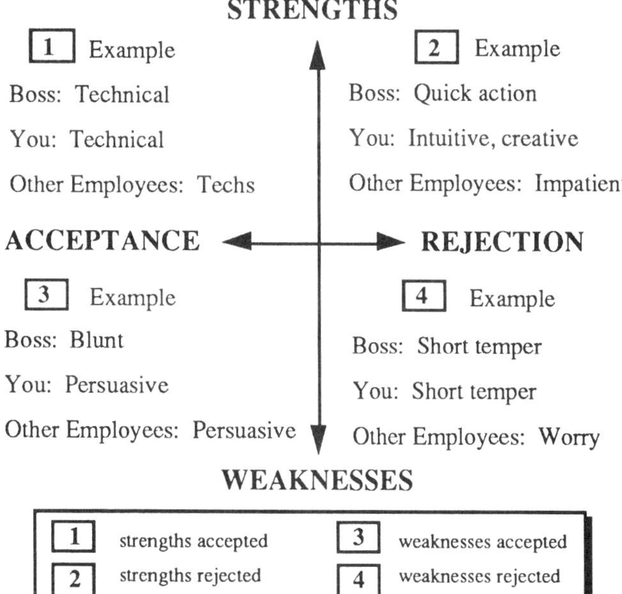

As we close this chapter, reflect on the 12 points of MBA and communication pressures that face people today in the workplace. Your leadership style helps to define an approach of flexibility in meeting various levels of employees. A way to summarize this chapter is to reexamine the two leadership concepts of the technical, results-oriented side and the people-oriented side of leadership. These two concepts are on a continuum.

Balance of Leadership

Task Orientation ◄————————► People Orientation
(Technical/Results)   (People)

This is a balancing act based on rapport, trust, competence, confidence, action, and development.

Analyze the dichotomy of a leader on the next page and relate it to your work associates.

THE DICHOTOMY OF A LEADER'S JOB

Technical Knowledge	*People Skills*
1. Up to date with specific content.	Development of self; keeping employees informed.
2. Ability to be used as a resource.	Personality to interact with employees, professionally and informally.
3. Decision maker and influencer.	Guide and develop employees to fulfill their needs, your needs, and the company's needs.
4. Task oriented.	Human relations oriented.
5. Help problem solve with employees and other managers.	Interact effectively with other managers and employees.
6. Identify levels of comprehension—you and others.	Work at the pace of others with patience and understanding.
7. Be self-motivated.	Be "other" directed.
8. Set priorities for yourself (e.g., work, family).	Help and guide others to organize and accomplish priorities.
9. Evaluate and communicate evaluation criteria; evaluate others.	Employees should be continually involved in the evaluation process; they should be able to evaluate themselves through management involvement.

How does this dichotomy change during organizational evolution and revolution? Organizational health can be measured through every level of leadership being held accountable to use the potential and talents in achieving the required technical and people results. All employees need to feel they are personal owners of the organization through a sense of challenge and commitment. They must be able to see themselves in the fabric of the organization. This occurs in different ways for each person because of their desires and level within the organization. Nevertheless, total organization worth can be achieved only when each employee is made to feel ownership of his or her job. This is accomplished through the leader's flexible understanding of the dichotomy of leadership.

You may want to reread this chapter just to reflect on your situation. **Give yourself credit for what you do well and have accomplished, and look at weaknesses or problems as great opportunities for self-development and growth.**

3

RELEARNING THE ART OF LEADERSHIP

Leadership and followership are crucial aspects of working within a team. Directing, guiding, and following within a team are critical for success of the team.

Applying knowledge is the essence of learning. Being able to affect the working environment and favorably control the outcome of job productivity is essential. As you work in the same environment, you can create a fresh outlook by changing your own and your employees' attitudes toward the conceptual and physical routine.

To create an effective working rapport through application, you should realize what needs to be accomplished in the short and long term. Be informed and make sure you have gathered and continue to gather information that will affect employee job productivity.

You should be "professional" within the working environment. A professional-working person should respect himself/herself, meet corporate expectations, and accomplish and fulfill a particular job responsibility within the corporate structure. Realize what can and cannot be done within a specific job because of individual, employee, and corporate parameters. Set priorities with what should be completed within a realistic time frame.

To "relearn" how to lead you must analyze your working and leadership styles. You can then better meet job expectations by building a team you can manage. Your effectiveness is dependent on each individual: the composite of the business team, management, each employee, your boss, and you. Therefore, it benefits everyone to guide and direct themselves to accomplish job expectations and improve job performance.

Leaders often do not realize that along with organizational authority comes the responsibility to develop employees so they will reach their potential while fulfilling job responsibilities. Today's leader must effectively guide employees to levels of productivity that will meet the needs of the organization, management, and individual employees. Building a strong rapport that is honest and productive should be the first objective of a team leader. Employees who respect and believe in themselves and their leader will work to achieve excellence.

A leader should not give orders to reassure positions within the corporation. Creating a team philosophy rather than an authoritarian philosophy can be beneficial for all parties. Job responsibilities can be better served by building a relationship of co-workers mutually reaching corporate *and* personal needs.

IT'S A NEW WAY OF THINKING

Every level of employment should be viewed as an important job. The organization cannot function without the president, who makes major decisions—nor can it continue without the refuse cleaners, who maintain healthy conditions. The corporation and all the working associates (CEO, management, support staff) have needs, and these needs and expectations should be identified and discussed openly by management with employees.

People should be treated on a positive, humanistic level rather than on a subordinate level. We all are people; we just have different job functions. This will enhance self-esteem, thereby improving productivity. One of the greatest mistakes a leader can make is *not* to utilize the potential of the employees in a company. The greatest advantage that a leader has is the ability to guide employees to achieve previously unattained maximum productivity. This guidance enables employees to achieve their potential through organizational and clearly established job responsibilities.

To ensure productivity and teamwork, leaders need to:

1. Openly and honestly communicate expected results. (No hidden agendas.)

2. Establish measurable methods of action.

3. Accept an honest evaluation by way of reassessing. Leaders should evaluate followers and followers evaluate leaders. This communicates a strong message.

4. Monitor performance to determine what is needed for each employee to achieve expected results.

5. Build a rapport to mutually satisfy personal, employee, and organizational needs.

Management is not a promotion—it is a responsibility to guide and develop yourself and employees to reach potentials and fulfill job responsibilities. Following are guidelines—Laws of Leadership—for creating an effective team.

LAWS OF LEADERSHIP

Communicate   Creating a safe environment in which to exchange ideas clearly; clarifying each individual's function and receiving feedback from the employees—feedback to feed the future. Share yourself through ideas. Are you asking the right questions to generate the process?

Coordinate   Asking the right questions; planning what is needed to successfully perform each job; knowing if the right person has been utilized to fulfill a job responsibility.

Organize   Using the right people at the right time to complete daily business plans. If you say it—do it. This will build trust (say=do).

Motivate   Establishing criteria that guide employees to work together; meeting individuals' potential and needs; helping them to understand the benefits for themselves; motivating them to get the maximum individual effort. Pull out motivation, inspire, and demonstrate.

Manage Resources	Properly utilizing employees and equipment; providing financial support, workday, and feedback on what is feasible. Be flexible to change. Are you utilizing all available resources?
Set Guidelines	Developing and establishing policies and procedures, financial restraints, corporate and human expectations, and realistic time frames, deadlines. Having the confidence in yourself to act and consistently reinforce.
Clarify Expectations and Methods of Action	Taking a realistic view of what should and could be expected for the corporation, customers, management, and employees and planning how to accomplish this realistic view.

CYCLE OF LEADERSHIP

The leadership cycle is only as effective as the limitations of the leader and team members. Therefore, it is essential that the rapport between the leader and employees be comprehensive beyond the job. You are not leading job descriptions, you are leading working people who have needs. Remember: Organizations don't have quality, people do—people drive organizations.

This cycle can help you identify and specifically work toward fulfillment of expected results. However, a reasonable time frame must be established to note accomplishment and reassessment.

Leaders and employees need to have an understanding of their strengths and weaknesses—opportunities for development. They should have an understanding, via the job description, of what is to be accomplished and how to accomplish it.

Leaders are accountable, along with team members, for the team's achieving measurable expectations. Following are guidelines for keeping the team on track.

1. Build a professional relationship with employees—work as equals—value their input. Always write salient points from your meetings for future reference.

2. As you set expected results, anticipate employee needs and skills. Team members will reflect the level of performance in which they perceive themselves. Employees' self-confidence levels will affect the establishment of realistic job expectations.

3. Focus formal conversations to establish corporate expectations in relationship to team members' job responsibilities. Establish employee methods of action by which expected results can be accomplished.

4. Help team members identify strengths and opportunities for development so that you can guide them and give feedback for development. These strengths and weaknesses should be honest assessments and should be unbiased toward any and every employee.

5. Make your reassessment of any procedure open, honest, respectful, and focused to discuss issues and content, not people.

GENERAL CONCEPTS FOR LEADERSHIP

Leaders are responsible for:

a) Maintaining and improving corporate health to a changing business environment; leading, taking action, effectively listening.

b) Developing themselves and other associates through interaction.

c) Being a team player: an active catalyst to stimulate action; being consistent, reinforcing the corporate attitude, culture, philosophy.

d) Developing employees; recognizing achievement, creating equity by treating employees fairly as individuals.

e) Analyzing general and specific business aspects; effectively communicating organizational and departmental goals and objectives.

f) Knowing the right questions, not just the answers (responses); being open, honest, and respectful.

g) Developing, carrying out, and implementing corporate policy on every level; holding everyone accountable for their jobs.

h) Creating improvement—innovative or adaptation—within the corporation; continual improvement means change.

i) Understanding the abilities and skills of each employee in relationship to their job responsibility; guiding the employees toward improved productivity and interaction and involvement, fairly and with equity; evaluating and interacting with each employee.

j) Identifying corporate, employee, and self needs on a continuing basis—as corporate needs change, so should management's philosophy; ensuring that direct reports follow appropriate rules and regulations.

k) Guiding employees to know the trade-offs of fulfilling their job responsibilities; ensuring self- and employee development through the challenges and achievements with the workplace.

l) Understanding the marketplace in relationship to the corporation and employee capabilities; soliciting and collecting employee suggestions; acting on the suggestions in some manner.

m) Meeting the needs of your internal (your manager, direct reports, peers) and external customers to assure responsible corporate representation; following corporate, state, and federal laws, regulations, and policies.

n) Setting short- and long-term expectations for self, employees, and the corporation; identifying career opportunities.

o) Adapting to business situations and circumstances; showing flexible leadership; eliciting participation among all employees.

p) Developing employees with potential; reprimanding, disciplining, and dealing fairly with employees who have problems.

q) Knowing when to say no or yes; employees will respect honesty even if they don't like the response.

r) Listening without judging, and making sound decisions; collecting information and expressing and addressing what you hear.

s) Evaluating without prejudice—being aware of your biases.

RESPONSIBILITIES

Responsibility—what you are willing to accept given your ability and the environment (available resources).

Team leaders have many responsibilities—to themselves *and* the team. Using the format below, list the **major** responsibilities of your position on a piece of paper. To the left of the number, list the employee(s) who affect(s) the performance of that particular responsibility.

Employee		**Your Responsibility**
_____________	1.	___________________
_____________	2.	___________________
_____________	3.	___________________
_____________	4.	___________________
_____________	5.	___________________
_____________	6.	___________________
_____________	7.	___________________
_____________	8.	___________________

What are your expectations of your job? Who is responsible for fulfilling those expectations?

Analyze the fulfillment of the job responsibilities that are listed. List your strengths in your job performance—what you satisfactorily fulfill—and your weaknesses—what you do not satisfactorily fulfill.

Reflect upon your job performance. What is expected?

<table>
<tr><td>Strengths</td><td>Opportunities
for Development</td></tr>
<tr><td>1. _______________</td><td>1. _______________</td></tr>
<tr><td>2. _______________</td><td>2. _______________</td></tr>
<tr><td>3. _______________</td><td>3. _______________</td></tr>
<tr><td>4. _______________</td><td>4. _______________</td></tr>
<tr><td>5. _______________</td><td>5. _______________</td></tr>
<tr><td>6. _______________</td><td>6. _______________</td></tr>
<tr><td>7. _______________</td><td>7. _______________</td></tr>
<tr><td>8. _______________</td><td>8. _______________</td></tr>
</table>

List any **changes** that you think would enhance your job performance (i.e., changing leadership style, communication, fewer direct reports, new workplace, equipment, networking).

1. ____

2. ____

3. ____

4. ____

5. ____

6. ____

WHAT DO YOU THINK?

Leaders should focus on strengths and opportunities for development to create an awareness and perspective of their job performance. Each of these concepts—Laws of Leadership, Cycle of Leadership, General Concept of Leadership—is paramount to the success of the team leader fulfilling the role and having a high job-performance level. How do you answer these questions?

1. Do you give support and recognition to employees?

2. Do you realize the concepts and values that you hold as true might not have the same meaning to other employees or be held corporate wide?

3. Do you have confidence in yourself to fulfill the job expectations, or do you constantly have anxiety about completing your work demands and employees' job expectations?

If there is an open rapport among team members, communication, productivity, and morale will improve. All employees need to feel wanted and be given credit when it is due. It is important for the leader to realize how the relationship with employees will affect the job-performance level. Conflict may arise when the parties are not properly communicating trust and the respect deserved. Leaders should develop an awareness and sensitivity toward building, gaining, and maintaining the respect of employees. This is not an easy task, but it is an attainable goal.

Leaders need to clearly state and focus employees to understanding and agreement. Conflict is easy to see and hear; however, agreement is too often assumed. An example is shipping of product. The manager explained the deadline clearly after a disagreement with marketing, but the product being shipped was assumed to be product A instead of B. The result was that the wrong product was shipped on time. Work often has to be redone because the message of what is to be accomplished is not clear. Make sure everyone knows what is agreed upon from a work action, productivity, and job responsibility point of view.

Leaders should reflect upon their thinking in relationship to the employee's thinking. There is no right or wrong answer to a philosophy of thinking, rather an acceptance of others'.

Acceptance of oneself and the people with whom you work will eliminate many biases. Everyone wins when a professional rapport is built upon mutual acceptance. It enhances job performance and helps meet corporate expectations.

Leaders should not continually perform the employees' jobs; they should guide them. An example: If the manager of an accounting department continually solves the monthly accounting report problems, the employees will not challenge and think for themselves. They will rely on the manager. The manager needs to give the employees the freedom to fail by entrusting confidence. Part of team development comes through failure. Failure can be a better learning-development situation than doing the employees' work for them.

When a working relationship incorporates the mutual trust of team leaders and members, the employees are less apprehensive in the performance of their jobs. Each employee has a unique working personality and style of communicating and thinking. The more that these characteristics can be accepted by the team leader, the more effectively the team will function. This is easy to discuss, but to build a successful business rapport that meets everyone's expectations is a long and arduous process. Even if employees work for minimum wage, they should not be looked down on; they still have needs. The leader can guide employees to accept and become part of an organization.

During a successful career, the three concepts of achieving recognition, understanding yourself with a positive self-regard, and becoming secure can develop through any position. The reason for introspection (self-analysis) of these points is to speed the process and maintain the levels of self-fulfillment as a leader.

As a teader, you should realize that you, as well as the employees, have needs. It is your job to meet the needs of management by leading others to accomplish established job expectations. The employees should be guided to realize that they can attain more than a paycheck through the corporation. They can develop friendships, become part of a team, be recognized for a job well done, and possibly be promoted. Therefore, it is essential to understand your own values, the corporate values, and the expectations and values of others.

ASSESSING *YOUR* LEADERSHIP NEEDS

To grow as a leader, you must constantly assess relationships, your working environment, and dreams of achievement. You need to create change intelligently to creatively improve. Time on task does not mean that you are better able to perform. If a mail person accurately delivers the mail the same way for 20 years, and another person creates new strategies to accurately deliver the mail more efficiently, who is the better mail person?

An assessment in terms of relationships and the working environment is very important. Burnout is a result of the routine, non-risk, unchallenging environment that is often created. The challenge is to create a new viewpoint, level of comprehension, and competence. Awareness of oneself—learning style, personality, mode of presenting—is the first step in assessing strong and weak points about ourselves. We must assess our goals and achievements within our own abilities. To fully understand ourselves is to reach out to fulfill our potential.

Ask yourself the following questions. Write your responses so you can reread them at a later date.

LEADER'S JOB DESCRIPTION

1. List your strongest job-related abilities.

---

2. How are your strongest abilities being utilized?

---

3. What are your specific duties?

---

4. Are you meeting all of your duties equally?

---

5. What are your personal job expectations?

---

6. What are *your* leader's expectations?

---

7. What areas of your performance would you want to change?

---

8. Can you successfully meet your job position? What are opportunities for you to develop?

YOUR JOB DESCRIPTION

From the collected information, write a job description that utilizes your strengths.

____

____

____

____

____

____

____

To relearn the art of leadership, you have to rethink what it is you do, and ask if it is now appropriate.

4

THE MEETING LEADER

So far we have been examining concepts of leadership within the workplace. This chapter is a concrete approach to applying these leadership ideas. Leaders: lead, communicate (face-to-face, phone), interact, interview, plan, and develop ideas. Most often, all of these activities occur in the setting of a meeting.

As a key function of organizational operations, a business meeting must have a focused direction . . . and an accomplished leader. This important function is more than a group coming together to express general opinions about the business climate. A business meeting's purpose should be to fulfill specific business expectations. Both immediate and long-term issues can and should be developed through the combined energies and personalities that are brought together in teams. Meetings can be a method through which a team, department, or division develops its influence in the company, firm, or corporate culture.

A business meeting has three basic functions:

1. To identify and specifically address business issues in a specified time frame.

2. To create a forum in which viewpoints are exchanged constructively and safely while addressing the identified business issues.

3. To establish a plan of action—short or long term. This action plan can be concrete (i.e., delegating responsibility to individuals) or scheduled for discussion at another meeting.

You've heard it all before. Quality begins in the boardroom. Efficient meetings mean more money. Statistical Process Controls (SPC) and Just In Time Inventory Analysis (JIT) are *the* methods of measurement.

But in a meeting, communication needs to be measured. Meetings should not conclude with everyone walking out stating, "This is what happened in the last meeting." Meeting agendas and actions need to be defined ahead of time. A meeting is an investment of time and money. These two concepts measured in a quality audit—time and cost ratio—are a deposit in a bank.

> Successful meetings follow this pattern:
>
> - Purpose was clear and achieved.
>
> - Expected results were clear and achieved.
>
> - Time frame was established and followed.
>
> - Agreement was reached on
>   follow-up action.

With the bank metaphor in mind, how much money did your organization lose today in wasteful meetings? How much interest was gained on your money through successful meetings? A method to gain interest on your deposit is to use a meeting agenda that is clear and concise. You must provide the big picture, purpose, specific expected results, and the degree of importance. This agenda can be given ahead of time, allowing speakers to come and go as needed, rather than being "captured" for the duration. The agenda also gives the team a format for follow-up action.

Let's look at the meeting agenda sample below. Analyze the format, beginning with title and each component. No meeting should be held without each member knowing the purpose, expected results, level of importance, and time frames. Reflect on your meetings.

MEETING AGENDA SAMPLE

Title of Meeting

Date ____

Time began _______ *Start your meeting off the hour, 1:15 or 1:45 p.m.* ____
(Too many things occur on the hour)

Time concluded ____

Place ____

People in attendance ____

Purpose ____

Expected results *(What is to be accomplished?)* _________________

Level of importance _____ *Crisis/Very important* _________________

1. Topic: _________________________   Decision(s) _______________
   Time to discuss: ____________   _______________________
   Discussion led by: __________   Action(s) to be taken ________
      ____

   Follow-up Questions: Time frame to accomplish
   1. What do we agree on   _______________________
   (from right column)?   _______________________
   2. How do you feel about it?   People involved (responsibilities)
      ____
      ____

2. Topic: _________________________   Decision(s) _______________
   Time to discuss: ____________   _______________________
   Discussion led by: __________   Action(s) to be taken ________
      ____

   Follow-up Questions: Time frame to accomplish
   1. What do we agree on   _______________________
   (from right column)?   _______________________
   2. How do you feel about it?   People involved (responsibilities)
      ____
      ____

The meeting leader is responsible for focusing and promoting discussion on follow-up actions and expected results. The meeting leader (or facilitator) is responsible for:

- identifying appropriate business issues or concerns.

- writing and distributing a pre-meeting agenda.

- setting a realistic, specific amount of time in which to hold the meeting and adhering to the agenda items within that time frame.

- procuring a room and necessary equipment.

- notifying the members of the meeting time and place.

- controlling the meeting and keeping it focused on the agenda items.

- giving an overview of what is to be accomplished, guiding the discussion on specific agenda issues, and summarizing the meeting.

- adjourning the meeting and distributing follow-up information to all necessary or appropriate people.

The leader's main responsibility is to remain in control of the energy or focus of the meeting. This person acts as a "team" leader who ensures that business issues or concerns are properly addressed. The leader dictates whether the agenda needs to be altered during the meeting because of lengthy, but appropriate, discussions.

Conflict within a meeting should not be avoided. It could clarify issues, but it must be handled effectively. An open, honest exchange of ideas can often generate creative solutions. The leader must identify concepts in conflict by paraphrasing and drawing all of the members into a productive sharing of ideas, while acknowledging resistance among members.

The leader needs to maintain the members' interest while focusing the meeting. This can be done only by giving everyone the opportunity to express his or her point of view, including pros and cons.

TIPS FOR IMPROVING MEETING EFFECTIVENESS

To be an effective meeting leader, you need to:

1. Create a pre-meeting agenda memo that lists attendees, issues to be discussed, and times.

2. Prepare an agenda. Make extra copies. Check all audiovisual equipment prior to the meeting.

3. Give an overview and focus on what is to be accomplished. Get a return on the meeting investment. Set the ground rules—are we here to inform or persuade?

4. Stand when you begin the meeting. (For an informal discussion, sit down after you call the meeting to order.) Position yourself at one end or near the middle of a conference table.

5. Allow top management the flexibility of not having to stay for the entire meeting. Permit them to address their specific issues and leave.

6. Anticipate and encourage group interaction to allow others a sharing of energy.

7. Collect the group's thoughts for distribution.

8. Share your viewpoints when no viewpoints on a topic are being shared.

9. Table issues with follow-up action for a later meeting.

10. Control the meeting to stay within the established time constraints; do not get sidetracked.

11. Before adjourning, make sure everyone clearly understands the agreement of follow-up actions from the meeting.

12. Follow up by distributing information to all appropriate attendees.

Being the leader of a meeting implies that you have confidence in your ability to control others in order to address issues. The meeting is being held for the discussion of business issues; it is not a time to review old acquaintances or talk about sporting events or to lose time. It provides information and utilizes attendees' energies (synergism) to raise the right questions to be answered. By raising the right questions, follow-up actions and positive business resolutions are developed.

Follow-up is essential in evaluating the effectiveness of the meeting. A meeting begins with its preparation and planning. After it is conducted, the meeting should be evaluated on both the interaction that occurred during the meeting *and* the follow-up action.

The follow-up action includes the distribution of minutes from the meeting to the appropriate executives, managers, professionals, support staff, and hourly employees. All employees (exempt and non-exempt) have a basic need to know, to be informed of policy and/or the action to be taken. If the purpose of a business meeting is to collect, share, and disseminate information, then *all* appropriate employees should be informed in order to keep them updated and to establish the expected results of the meeting.

BUILDING RAPPORT

How do you want to be perceived—as a meeting member or facilitator? The meeting actually begins with an agenda before you greet the members as they come into the room. The meeting lasts after adjournment through follow-up actions. You can set the climate of the meeting at this time. If it is the first meeting, have the members introduce themselves. If the group has met previously, introduce only the new members.

Be "other" directed. Think about the group's interests. Solicit ideas from participants who are withdrawn. Present the agenda items at a pace and level of comprehension suitable to the members. Remember: You wrote the agenda; stick to it!

Create interest via your voice and visuals. Vary your rate of speech (slow at times, quick at times) and, if possible, move around the room. Concentrate on your vocal inflection as a means of creating excitement. Make eye contact with each group member. Don't focus on or stare at the highest-ranking authority person.

Know the agenda and stick to it. Be aware of any new information regarding agenda items. Keep the meeting on track. Interject strongly, if needed, to keep the meeting flowing. Do not let the meeting go on past the time committed to in the pre-meeting agenda memo.

PROCESS VS. CONTENT

A meeting should have substantive concepts or topics of interest to most members. However, no matter what the content, the manner in which it is processed determines the outcome of the meeting. It is not just the content of the meeting, but also the discussion and interaction that take place during the meeting that determine the results of the members.

As the meeting leader, you should plan to control and stimulate an open sharing of ideas among the members. Create a safe environment, taking into consideration the attending members, situation, and agenda topics. You should begin by building trust and removing barriers. Establish actions for and from the meeting. Interject to control the pace; however, do not stifle creativity. Encourage open, honest, and respectful communication by modeling those communicative concepts. Help identify roles for each participating member, even if they will attend only one meeting. Make members feel a part of the meeting by encouraging them to share experiences that could lead to future actions.

Sharing ideas helps to keep the process of the meeting ongoing, no matter what the topic. To be a successful meeting leader, you must continually monitor the content and how it is processed (group interaction). Maintaining a safe environment with the support of everyone in the room is essential to having successful meetings. Encourage the group to problem solve and take advantage of group interaction energies. As a meeting leader/facilitator, you must ensure that knowledge (content) is processed in a manner that is *safe* and *productive* for all involved in the meeting.

Positive Interaction

The purpose of a meeting is to have a positive outcome; supportive and/or corrective action can and should be addressed. A positive outcome from a meeting does not mean that the actions or discussions were all of a supportive nature; corrective actions and discussions can produce positive results in a meeting. Positive outcomes do not preclude corrective or possibly hostile statements. As part of the processing, you should support discussion of a supportive and corrective nature. Supportive and corrective discussions are positive because both styles of interaction represent an open sharing of ideas. The words "negative meeting" or "negative comments" should not be used. If supportive and/or corrective discussions require follow-up action, they should be presented in a positive way and clearly understood by all the members.

Summary

The process that takes place during a meeting is as important as the content being presented. Involve all of the members in order to get their viewpoints. Create a safe environment and encourage and stimulate discussion, note taking, and follow-up action. Stick to agenda items and conclude the meeting within the given time constraints. These methods for conducting a meeting create the ideal that a meeting leader should strive to attain. By meeting the needs of the members of the group, you meet your own needs as a leader/facilitator of the meeting.

TIME MANAGEMENT IN MEETINGS

Time management is the utilization of periods of time in order to meet necessary priorities. This is accomplished by effectively using agenda times, problem solving given the changing environments and available resources, and effectively motivating others to focus their energies on the same necessary priorities.

Following are the most important actions you can take to ensure an efficient meeting:

1. Develop an action plan that coincides with the agenda, based on the participants, speakers, topics, and situation. Example: Introduce the budget speaker. If appropriate, interject when there are eight or nine minutes to go by asking for a summary. Tell the meeting members what follow-up actions need to be taken.

2. Reflect on what needs to be accomplished; write your thoughts.

3. Focus energies on fulfilling your responsibilities in the action plan and controlling and stimulating interaction in the meeting.

4. Establish a time frame in which the follow-up responsibilities need to be accomplished.

5. Problem solve to achieve time efficiency. Members should clearly know their roles in accomplishing tasks in the anticipated time frame.

6. Analyze your greatest time problems (e.g., outspoken member) and plan for them. Clearly establish the ground rules for time requirements.

OBSTACLES TO EFFECTIVE MEETINGS

Being an effective meeting leader requires exceptional interpersonal and time management skills and cooperation. Yet, you also must be prepared for and capable of handling unforeseen interruptions and obstacles. Following are some tips for "managing" events outside the meeting circle:

Interruptions/Phone Calls

Do not permit calls in the room during the meeting. Arrange in advance to have incoming calls for meeting members transferred. Unexpected interruptions should not be tolerated. Managers/Secretaries should not be permitted to disrupt the meeting unless it is an emergency.

Disrupter

A disrupter is a meeting member who interrupts the progress of others by introducing topics not originally on the agenda or who continually repeats ideas unnecessarily. The meeting leader should control the meeting and the disrupter by standing, interjecting, and refocusing the meeting on agenda items. Allow the person to speak until he or she repeats the issue. Collect information; even write the points on a flip chart. This will paraphrase and give recognition to what the disrupter said. Now you can state when you want to address the issue and control the meeting.

Hostile Person

This obstacle is a person who comes to the meeting angry. Listen and show concern, care, and understanding. Make eye contact; show interest. You develop team interaction by supporting others in a professional way. This does not mean you agree. Be empathetic and honest. Acknowledge and restate what you heard. Respond respectfully.

Conflict

There are many variables that can influence any and all group processing, including conflict. Many times it is *how* you say something rather than *what* you say that will resolve conflicts and other aspects of the team interaction. Consider who is there. Also, realize that conflict is an important aspect of team development. It can be used in a positive way to clarify different viewpoints.

Organizational Problems

Organizational problems result from poor pre-planning and preparation, not knowing who is to do what, and by letting someone else take control of the meeting. Be forthright; proactively address issues. Clearly identify the role or function of each member in attendance, even if the member is attending only one meeting. Use each and every meeting member as a resource.

Time

Set a realistic schedule so there is enough time to comfortably address agenda items. Time lost cannot be regained. Keep in mind people's energy levels and allot time accordingly. If you've scheduled a meeting for two hours or longer, build in time for a 10-15 minute break—it will refresh meeting members.

Agenda Development

An agenda is not simply a list of topics. The agenda should include the topics to be discussed, actions to be taken, and a timetable. Prepare and distribute an agenda that lists topics and allows room for note taking prior to the meeting. (Sample agendas appear at the end of this chapter.)

Poor Interaction

Poor interaction among the members should not be permitted to continue. This is often a sign that there is a lack of interest or trust among the members. Address the issues of trust, how to build interest, and how to work together. Discuss the importance of working together to achieve a common goal. To begin the discussion, ask questions and address them yourself—ask if others have thought about this topic. This is a practical way to begin the discussion.

Maturity Level of the Group

Group members mature as they work together. The first meeting members have together will be polite and courteous. Subsequent meetings bring about the development of small groups (cliques) or supporters within the group. The cliques and/or supporters eventually develop into the influencers and the decision makers within the group. Use the maturity level of the group by assigning tasks, having different members work together, recognizing each member's role and responsibility. Each group, based on the personality composite of its members, has a unique personality. The leader should learn to control the group's interest and maturity level (based on the topic and situation).

Stress

Stress is universal, but its causes vary. Know the breaking point of the members of the group. The possible causes of stress include time constraints, budget problems, interruptions, personality conflicts, and a need to be doing something else. Discuss and honor individual causes of stress within the meeting. Remember to take appropriate breaks.

Ineffective Listening

Listening and speaking are of equal importance in effective communication. The purpose of communication is to disseminate, share, and collect information. The effective listener unbiasedly collects information in the manner in which it is presented. No one can listen and speak simultaneously. Don't permit side discussions; they disrupt the process. If it isn't politically wise to address the side discussion, make sure you paraphrase and summarize.

The information should be interpreted first on the speaker's terms, and then the listener's. The main resultant of effective communication is the mutual understanding of the speaker's and listener's terms. Mutual understanding implies that the communication is interpreted on a mutual level of comprehension. Presenter and listener understand it in the same manner. The purpose of effectively speaking and listening is to establish a mutual result from the interaction of creating partners (speaker/listener) in communication. Check periodically for understanding and clarify as needed.

Disagreement with Expectations

When verbal and written expectations for the group are not clearly established, the group cannot utilize its combined strengths.

Discuss, with input from all of the members, agenda topics of business issues and/or concerns. Create a plan of action by which to measure the accomplishment of the established group expectations. The best way for you (as the meeting leader) and the group to have a sense of accomplishment is to clearly define what it is you want to accomplish and how you will measure the progress of that accomplishment.

DEVELOPING AN AGENDA

Following are some guidelines and recommendations for developing agendas. The more you prepare for a meeting, the greater the likelihood that it will be a success.

1. Identify business issues and/or concerns.

    a) Target a group of employees for their opinions with a one-page questionnaire.
    b) Ask people who will be in attendance for agenda items.
    c) Choose topics that you feel need to be discussed.

2. Set a realistic time frame.

    a) There is no set time for every meeting. However, realize that the longer the meeting, the more the members will mentally drift to their desk work.
    b) Establish or estimate the time that would be appropriate to discuss the issue. (Many issues can be discussed within an hour's time if the agenda is followed.)
    c) Clearly state the purpose of the meeting. What are the expected results from holding this meeting?
    d) If you can conclude a meeting ahead of time, you can attain greater buy-in and commitment. Agree on follow-up action.

3. Anticipate and address agenda issues.

    a) Find the right person with the facts.
    b) Invite guest speakers to address specific issues. (Guests do not have to stay for the entire meeting.)

4. When possible, distribute the agenda prior to the meeting date. This should give most members a chance to schedule the meeting and prepare mentally, as well as gather needed material.

5. Develop and use a pre-meeting agenda memo.

TIPS FOR PROCESSING THE AGENDA

1. Three-hole punch the agenda so meeting attendees can easily store it in a binder.

2. Encourage note taking on the agenda sheet.

3. Begin each meeting with a follow-up from the last meeting, if needed.

4. Do not try to do too much in a given period of time. Only so much information can be collected, shared, and disseminated within a meeting.

5. Create a relaxed atmosphere, but remember that *you* should be the controlling influencer.

6. Check and use the meeting agenda as a guide.

7. Conclude your meeting at or before the specified meeting time.

PRESENTING TO INFLUENCE

Planning—Create a Focus, Don't Waste Time

- Set your meeting off the hour (e.g., 9:15 a.m. or 10:45 a.m. rather than 9:00 a.m. or 10:00 a.m.).
- Establish time concluded.
- Know the place and get there early.
- Know all who will be involved.
- Be proactive, supportive, and innovative; get everyone involved and foster an open dialogue.
- Know what you want to accomplish and measure the results.

Overview—What is Going to Occur? Be Flexible.

- Greeting: possible small talk
- Topic(s): speak to the right people
- Purpose: expected results, level of importance of meeting
- Set ground rules (time, questions, handouts)
- Benefits of the meeting (why should people listen?)

Body—Depending on What You Want to Accomplish

- Ask general questions. Listen: collect information and need.
- Identify and clarify *"customer"* needs.
- Present and bridge your information (facts) and needs with *"customer"* needs.

Summary—No New Information Given Except for Questions

- State, *"In summary . . ."* or *"In conclusion . . ."*
- Restate important points—paraphrase.
- Identify agreement and possible problems.
- Discuss and agree on follow-up action.
- Get a decision.
- Establish individual responsibilities for action.

FOLLOWING UP ON A MEETING

Acknowledge and discuss real business needs. Listen to *what* is said, not just what you *want* to hear. *Listen without rebuttal.*

- Identify the business issues to be addressed. Target attending members for their concerns.
- Include the right people who have the pertinent information to address the issues.
- Identify issues and state them clearly.
- Have the group discuss possible actions and summarize.
- Devise a sequential action plan (Step 1, Step 2, etc.).
- Develop a realistic time frame in which to carry out and complete the action plan of the meeting.
- Create guidelines for the assessment of the actions taken on the decisions.
- Schedule follow-up action on the agenda for the next meeting.
- Distribute minutes from the meeting within two days or less.

SUMMARY

You will have to call on all of your leadership skills to create a meeting that will generate and promote an open exchange for all of the attendees. A meeting needs to ensure the following points:

- Establish a safe environment that will foster a sharing of ideas to build rapport and trust.
- Explain purpose (Why?), expected results, and level of importance.
- Establish direction (business objectives, the desired results, outcomes) and topics to be discussed.
- Establish a plan of action and procedures, and implement that process; establish a time frame.
- Develop alternatives; be flexible and able to deal with changes; listen to and openly discuss ideas; share your positional power, prestige, influence, and authority; involve everyone.
- Listen effectively. Understand others first. Speak one at a time; communicate. To influence, you have to understand other people's ideas to establish a mutual understanding.
- Discuss issues. Clarify your understanding. Come to an agreement.
- Take action.

5

Taking the Work out of Teamwork

> Together Energy Achieves More.

The process of individuals coming together to create a unique sharing of energies toward a common goal, in an open, honest, trusting, and respectful manner, thereby achieving expected results through unified actions.

There are many differences between teams and groups. Coming together to accomplish a specific mission does not mean that you have created a team. A group is composed of individuals coming together to discuss issues or to inform. Teams build upon the group concept by defining roles for the individual members, utilizing individual strengths, and nurturing synergism (working together) to create a unified plan of action in order to achieve identified results.

A team, like a symphony orchestra, must work together. To function harmoniously, team members must realize that the purpose of the team is not greater than, but equal to, the functioning process.

The first step should be to write the team's purpose/mission and its responsibility to the organization. Identifying expected results will create organization and give direction in which the team could work. The second step should be to define the strengths each person brings to the table. It is important to know why each person was asked to be a member of the team. This should be stated openly to support each individual and let every member be recognized. Third, each person should accept a role showing involvement and commitment. The team members should discuss issues and write an action plan that will create change based on the expected results, individual strengths, involvement, and commitment. Results will occur through the combined strengths of the team members performing, in their own styles, their team responsibilities. After the general responsibilities for the team are established, specific individual responsibilities should be established utilizing the right member for the task.

Individuals' strengths change during the team process (synergism, shared energy) because each person can become a catalyst that sparks other members' creative awareness. Often, members of a team may be strengthened because of the energy level that is produced by the group. Therefore, it is essential that each team member build a trusting, open, honest, and respectful relationship with the other members. Trust is being able to rely on one another. Openness is speaking what you are thinking rather than playing political games. Honesty is stating the facts clearly without purposeful ambiguity. Respectfulness is realizing that each person in the team deserves equal dignity.

Each team member performs a unique role by influencing the team through effective communication. The individual team member can communicate via many roles, such as informer, supporter, friend, supervisor, devil's advocate, innovator, representative, etc. These different roles can produce an environment that creates a cohesiveness that influences the team toward action. As a team matures, individual actions and expected roles solidify.

Developing individual expected roles is both a plus and a minus. Role expectations created through job responsibilities (position) and the fulfilling of responsibilities can cause conflicts. Sometimes, when group expectations of a certain individual's role are either exceeded or not fulfilled, conflicts might occur. Conflict can occur when a member is perceived to exceed his role expectations or authority. The same is true if a member does not fulfill group expectations. For example, the leader of the team (which is often the first and most clearly defined role) is challenged by takeover. If someone challenges the leader's expected role responsibility or authority, conflict might and often will occur.

As team and individual roles and characteristics are developed and utilized, team members should remember that ideas (issues) are equal to the processing (interpersonal skills) of those ideas by the team. Many times issues are tabled or lost because they are presented by the wrong team member, exceeding the member's authority or role. Therefore, strategic planning is important to know how to present issues. Present ideas in a way team members will respond favorably. Use visuals and diagrams. Explain and outline content and follow up with handouts. Ideas are accepted or rejected in their presentment, which creates the perception of "satisfying expectations" about the content and presentation.

Each member should present ideas in a positive way that will help to guide the team toward its goal(s). Other members of the team should respond appropriately, as should the team leader. If the perceived leader does not focus and direct the strengths of the members, the team will not develop until a new leader evolves as a decision maker. The team should encourage debate between its members in a safe environment to promote a well-thought-out plan of action that will accomplish the expected results.

Following are guidelines for team development and nurturing:

1. Establish the purpose of the team and determine its responsibility to the organization.

2. Discuss and agree upon expected results and time frames through group consensus.

3. Discuss strategies and methods that will accomplish the expected results.

4. Discuss and assume roles to establish self-worth as team members. Discuss how each role will help lead to the expected results.

5. Recognize the leaders, decision makers, advisors, and influencers within the team.

6. Discuss and accept the team's process for communication and working styles (e.g., analytical, structured, random, flexible, big picture).

7. Create a safe environment to encourage trusting, open, honest, and respectful discussions.

8. Discuss and encourage individual perspectives rather than promoting intellectual incest ("yes" people).

9. Continually foster rapport building among team members (e.g., breakfast, lunch, dinner, social meetings).

10. Recognize individual achievements within the team to promote credibility.

11. Involve the entire team in the problem-solving and decision-making process by encouraging input from each member.

12. Strive to work through deadlocked issues, thereby developing intellectual team growth.

The goal of team development is the interpersonal rapport of coming together to achieve expected results. By identifying the individuals you are involved with as a group or a team, you can determine your commitment, motivation, roles, and expectations.

Let's examine in detail the 12 points of what constitutes a team and how a team should work.

1. **Establish the purpose of the team and determine its responsibility to the organization.** Defining the purpose of the team is the most important aspect of team building. Why? It gives direction. Purpose indicates why the team was formed and begins to outline a plan of action. Purpose clarifies immediate actions and what is to be accomplished. It is the big picture or overview of what is to occur.

Example: *The purpose of this team is to examine the employee benefits program and make recommendations.* The second concept in this first point is the team's relationship and responsibility to the larger organization. This is a point that is often forgotten. Teams should fulfill an organizational responsibility. Can an organization have responsibilities? Yes! Those responsibilities are mandated by boards of directors, CEOs, presidents, managing partners, etc. These broad responsibilities give direction, set standards and traditions, and in a very real sense, set the corporate culture, or as Warren Bennis refers to it, "social architecture."

The combination of purpose and responsibility will give the team focused direction and ownership as well as involvement in the organization. This last point is something that is missing from most organizations. Research indicates that employees often feel alone and do not have a sense of involvement or connection to the organization. They do not connect what they do on a day-to-day basis and relate that to the fulfillment of an organizational responsibility. An ingredient of motivation is reminding employees of the benefit of their service, and how that service adds to the value of the organization. It is important for the team and its individual members to have this understanding of connection. Establishing purpose and direction and obtaining clear understanding of responsibility to the organization—and how that meets and fulfills the organization's need and responsibility—can help to motivate, encourage, and give a sense of purpose to the team.

2. **Discuss and agree upon expected results and time frames through group consensus.** Many people think teams are a forum for presenting and discussing differing viewpoints. However, it is agreement, not conflict, that should drive teams. Agreement must be asked for, discussed, and clearly identified. Agreement for the sake of consensus, though, creates problems because people may perform actions contrary to the needs or desires of the group. Jerry Harvey in his Abilene Paradox explains that groups often will take action no one really believes in because there is no clarity of purpose, or to "connect" the team to fulfilling an organizational responsibility.

   Everyone in the team needs to have a clear understanding as to the expected results. What is the product that the team is to produce? What is to be accomplished? Often it is probably best to work backwards. Know what is expected as the final result and develop a system or process to achieve it. Confusion comes into play when members of the team do not know or understand what needs to be accomplished—what are the desired results. An agenda of realistic actions and times needs to be expressed and agreed upon. Arriving at the expected results and time frames through consensus means that everyone has expressed their viewpoint, and the team then establishes agreement as to realistic results within a given period of time.

   Coming to agreement through consensus makes each member feel involved and part of the team. This openness is what will encourage honesty, respect, and trust in the team and begin to establish a safe environment for further discussions.

3. **Discuss strategies and methods that will accomplish the expected results**. To meet the goal(s) of the team you must develop a plan that specifically outlines how to accomplish and achieve the expected results. The methods fill in the plan or strategy with specific action on the part of each team member. Involvement is critical; each member must have input to succeed. This will then give recognition to each member, and the team can and will function as a collection of synergistic (shared energy) mind. The concept of symbiosis is that each member supports each other in a powerful way to achieve results on time, within budget, and to the team's satisfaction.

4. **Discuss and assume roles to establish self-worth as team members. Discuss how each role will help lead to the expected results**. Once the first three points are properly implemented within a team, individual roles will help drive the team process. By establishing the purpose, agreeing on expected results, and discussing strategies, each member has the opportunity to establish his or her role in the team. Finding a place in the team allows each member to contribute and build his or her sense of recognition and add to the synergistic and dynamic relationship that occurs in a team.

5. **Recognize the leaders, decision makers, advisors, and influencers within the team.** Each team member probably will assume several roles during the team process. The leader is not necessarily the highest organizational authority within the team. If you analyze the dynamics of a team you'll see that various leaders will emerge. What are the signs? The leader fields questions,

addresses issues quickly, and directs or focuses the discussion. This can occur with several or all of the group members.

However, decision makers are typically content experts or the highest-ranking person in attendance. The person perceived to be the decision maker usually fulfills that responsibility within the team.

Advisors and influencers differ. An advisor informs and provides updates and presents data or information. The influencer goes beyond informing. The influencer presents information with the intent of persuading the other team members to agree, adopt ideas, and support the points presented. This concept of influence is subtle. It differs from manipulation in that to influence or persuade, one shares or overshares information. To manipulate someone you withhold information.

Example: A junior faculty member was asked to write and present a paper. He did so and submitted it to the chairman of the department. The chairman put a new title page indicating that the paper came from the department that he headed. The junior faculty member was livid, and stormed in to see the chairman whereupon he said, "But you are part of the department; calm down." This did not calm the junior faculty member; he felt used. This is a classic case of manipulation. The chairman knew the paper was to come from the department; the junior member did not.

On the other hand, influence is a clear sharing of inner thoughts in such a way that the other team members emotionally buy in to and adopt those ideas as their own. This should also clarify the difference of the perceived leader of the team who influences, rather than dictates to, the team. These four roles are critical within the dynamics and development of the team.

6. **Discuss and accept the team's process for communication and working styles (e.g., analytical, structured, random, flexible, big picture).** Often, teams immediately discuss action content—who will do what—without addressing the humanistic interactive process. The best suggestion here is to periodically discuss how the team works together. How do you process information? Do you overanalyze, examine the big picture, or wander from topic to topic? Or is it structured down to the minute? The correct approach is a combination of all four styles, considering what is to be accomplished, the purpose of the meeting, time frames, and the expectations of team members.

There is no one way to approach team processes. Each of these approaches is appropriate based on the team's needs, wants, and expectations at a particular time.

7. **Create a safe environment to encourage trusting, open, honest, and respectful discussions.** The concept of "safe" environment often cannot be put into words; it must be recognized and embodied. Do you know anyone who can say, "Okay, this is a safe environment. Expose your deepest thoughts about me and the organization—trust me."?

You will be able to identify a safe environment by how well each person in the team expresses his or her ideas. If the other members actively listen without immediately responding.

Safe environments develop with time and it is each member's responsibility to support a safe environment. Safety is created by *not* discussing points out of context or confiding in others outside the team; by showing support and openly expressing and exchanging ideas—this also builds trust and honesty. Time is the only method to achieve various levels of safety, trust, honesty, and respect. It generally is based on follow-up action. You said you would, and did. We all have certain levels of safety, trust, openness, honesty, and respect with every person. However, based on the rapport and that person's actions, our levels increase or decrease.

These concepts are easy to express in words, but it is difficult to achieve these points among individuals within the team and the team as a whole. Human nature is that people want to take charge or get their points across, or want things done as they see it. All of these actions inhibit the growth of safe, honest, open trust in any relationship. Remember that follow-up action, fulfilling what you say, and giving people the opportunity to express their ideas while you listen will build these concepts.

8. **Discuss and encourage individual perspectives rather than promoting intellectual incest ("yes" people).** Group thinking can present problems. Each person in the team is accountable to present his or her ideas whether in support or

disagreement. This is the only way a team will take full advantage of the creativity and resource within the team. If not, the goals of the team might be compromised. Passive persistence could emerge (i.e., "Okay. If that's what you want."). This is not productive for the team. Another hindrance to individual thinking can come from fear of a strong leader. For example: J. F. Kennedy in the Cuban missile crisis had to tell his advisors he wanted the truth—not what they thought he wanted them to say. He learned this through the disaster of the Bay of Pigs incident.

9. **Continually foster rapport building among team members (e.g., breakfast, lunch, dinner, social meetings).** It is important that team members continue to expand their interactions. Discuss issues out of and away from the team's formal atmosphere. They need to learn more than what is involved in the specific function of the team. People within a team often are acquainted with or friendly with others within the team. Informal rapport building is a way to build trust, create a safe environment, help others, and explain why people feel the way they do.

10. **Recognize individual achievements within the team to promote credibility.** We really don't celebrate or give recognition to others when they accomplish projects or tasks. Recognition is a motivator and a way to let the other team members know that they are appreciated for their efforts and accomplishments. This should not be phony but a sincere effort to recognize contribution and accomplishments of the individual team members. Many times informal recognition such as buying

someone lunch, sending a memo to the person's boss, or simply thanking the person for helping, go a long way toward building a stronger team.

11. **Involve the entire team in the problem-solving and decision-making process by encouraging input from each member.** If you have created an open, honest, trusting environment, it becomes easier for individuals to contribute, and a team cannot function without creative input. A creative team uses all available resources—people and equipment, allowing everyone to share information.

    Problem solving implies that problems—as well as strengths for handling them—have been identified. The way to solve a problem is through input from others. Plan for creative output (brainstorming, open discussion, memos, etc.). This can be accomplished if all resources are tapped.

12. **Strive to work through deadlocked issues, thereby developing intellectual team growth.** Before a conflict arises, identify methods of problem solving or discussing disagreement. Again, this refers to the sharing of ideas and creating a safe environment. Discuss how to work together before barriers or alliances are established to support one side or the other. By discussing how you will work together, your team will function more efficiently and effectively.

    In conclusion, these 12 points are critical to forming and having a team work together effectively. (The next section will look at a variation or stages that teams go through in achieving these 12 points.)

QUALITY TEAMS

The effectiveness and efficiency of a team can be measured through time and action, which equal cost. Both of these everyday occurrences, time and action, equal the process of generating and losing productivity, cost. They are the foundation of work on a daily basis. If we believe what Drucker, Juran, and Deming say about quality, then we have to break it into the smallest units. The quality process is the effective and efficient use of time and action.

Vince Lombardi, the great football coach, is attributed to have said that football is a game of inches. Productive work is a game of time and action—utilizing realistic periods of time to achieve through appropriately applied action.

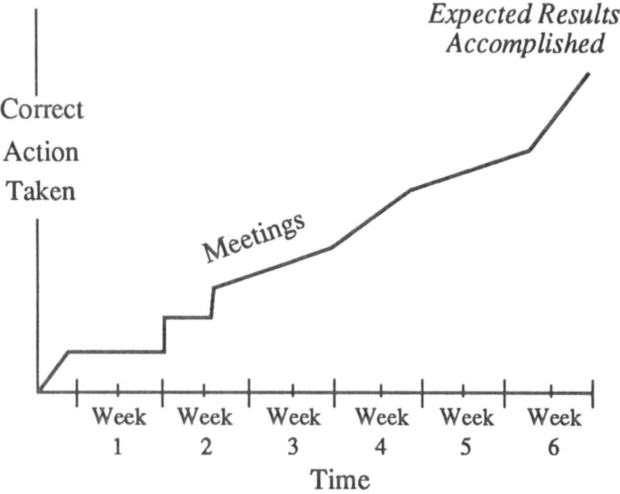

Let's examine a model of how teams develop. This model indicates that to become productive, teams, just like people, go through developmental stages. These various stages are greatly influenced by the make-up of the team. One of the most popular models was developed by Tuckman (1965): Stage 1—**Forming** (testing and dependence); Stage 2—**Storming** (conflict); Stage 3—**Norming** (team cohesion); and Stage 4—**Performing** (team productivity).

A team has a personality just like a person, though the team has a personality composed of several individuals. Cattell (1951) used the word "syntality" to define the personality of a team. He focused on the interactive ability of the group, level of energy, and leadership which would obviously lead to its followership.

Bion (1961) had another model: Stage 1—**Flight**; Stage 2—**Fight**; Stage 3—**Unite**.

Golembiewski (1962): Phase 1—Establish a **Hierarchy**; Phase 2—**Conflict** and Frustration; Phase 3—**Growth** and Security and Autonomy; Phase 4—Structuring in Terms of **Work-Task**.

These models all support the concept of coming together. They establish a pecking order or, through conflict, establish purposes that begin to work together.

The last model to be analyzed was developed by Charrier (1974). He called it "Cogs Ladder." This identifies the stages or maturing that a team goes through to become a viable and working entity. Let's take a closer look at Cogs Ladder.

Stage 1—Polite Stage. This is the time to get acquainted. It is a very congenial stage, a "please and thank you period." Just like meeting someone for the first time, everyone wants to make a fine impression. Each person begins to feel the other people out. Who are these people? What do they do? Why are they here?

Stage 2—Why Are We Here? The team begins to explain what members are supposed to do. Direction of work energy is explained: goals, objectives, purpose, and what is to be accomplished are discussed. At this point, two things can occur—conflict or agreement. Most often conflict creates the clarity because agreement is seldom asked for and required. What needs to occur is a clear understanding of what the team agrees to accomplish. This ensures that action contrary to the desire of the team does not occur.

Stage 3—Bid for Power. A development of cliques and a power base is established. A process of power, influence, and competence emerges. There is a strong bid for people to get their point established; the leader begins to emerge. (Bennis and Nanus 1985, p. 39.)

Leaders articulate and define what has previously remained implicit or unsaid; then they invent images, metaphors, and models that provide a focus for new attention. By doing so, they consolidate or challenge prevailing wisdom. In short, an essential factor in leadership is the capacity to influence and organize meaning for the members of the organization.

This is a critical stage because it establishes a work process that, for many teams, might last the entire life of the team. The other real factor is that organizational position or authority is no guarantee for leadership. Any team member can and will emerge as a leader when appropriate (e.g., expertise, levels of confidence, and support).

Stage 4—Construction. The team begins to work together based on the established process of dynamic interaction. In many cases, this is simply the unconscious processing of the agenda or work; however, this is a stage that needs to be discussed— how to work productively given time constraints and team action.

Stage 5—The Team Stage. The competence level of the team syntality may fluctuate depending on the agenda. The team uses synergism or team energy to process and develop a level of productivity.

All of these stages are crucial. They define the character of the team, and how the members will build from each other and achieve more collectively than as individuals.

TWO TYPES OF TEAMS

Leader-dependent Team

This is a team that has come together to be informed by the leader. The leader's main objective is not to influence or persuade the team; the leader simply presents the policy or procedure. The leader's job is to disseminate information, clarify issues, and ask questions as to the level of understanding by the team members. Other activities include pinpointing problems, facilitating understanding, encouraging questions, and clarifying information.

To be effective, the leader must be prepared and clearly know the information. If the leader tries to "wing it," the meeting can be seen as a waste of time and could lower the team's expectations of and confidence in the leader. The team needs to exhibit active listening skills and openly clarify points so there is a mutual understanding of the information, how it can be used, and what follow-up action is needed.

Many times, as the team leader explains the information, he/she will reach a deeper understanding of the information. This type of team formation emphasizes the leader being able to create an environment that will promote learning through questions. This "relaxed" environment requires the leader to be personable and capable of eliciting involvement.

Task-dependent Team

An example of a task team is the corrective action or creative team. The task-dependent team is involved in a project or activity to address specific points. The most important aspect of this team is working together to achieve a predetermined goal.

This team must remember to define responsibilities for each team member. Once the team clearly identifies its goals, it needs to assess how the members will work together and how to measure the results. Keep in mind that the true control of the group comes from an organizational authority who wants some specific action to occur.

For example, the corrective action team explores issues to address problems because this is a way to enhance productivity, service, or working relationships. Many corporations use task-dependent teams as part of their quality process. During this process it is important to prevent subteams, groups, or cliques from forming and trying to dominate. This team must establish and clarify its business objectives, have motivated members, establish a strategy to measure progress, and make sure all of its members participate.

If there has been no designated leader, then a leader needs to emerge. Most often leaders emerge because of knowledge, competence, and the confidence to lead. When a leader emerges, it is important that the team support and follow. Most often in a task team, more than one person will emerge as a leader. This can be a very creative way for the team to develop. If there is a designated leader, then that person needs to realize when to step back and become a follower, because of other team members' expertise and ability to lead during certain topic discussions.

ROLES WITHIN THE TEAM

The forces that occur in a team are sometimes mysterious and not easily explained. The unassuming become soapbox lecturers, and the "wait till we get to the meeting" person never says a word.

As mentioned earlier, Jerry Harvey in his Abilene Paradox points out that sometimes teams can take action contrary to the thoughts of the individuals. According to Harvey, the problem is not to resolve conflict, for there is no conflict, but rather the absence of agreement. It is the failure to come to agreement, and not necessarily conflict, that causes problems within a team. Team members take risks, initiate action and openly discuss issues to come to agreement. How can a team of individuals work together and create a unified body of energy?

Let's start at the beginning by examining the study of groups and their internal dynamics and interactions.

Kurt Lewin is considered the founder of modern-day group dynamics. He co-established the Field theory, which is a method of analyzing relationships and interactions. The Field theory is related closely to Gestalt theory, which states that the sum of the parts does not equal the whole. People put into a group will act in ways they might never have acted alone. The experience of the group empowers people to act because of the interacting elements or dynamics within the group.

The Field theory examines the environment and states that people come to interact in the group according to their past life experiences (knowledge and social behavior) and dynamics of the group such as: time of day, length of meeting; perceived importance of the meeting; frustration, tension, or relaxation levels; perceived power of the group; and the shared energy or synergism. There are two basic causes for people to conform in a group setting: first, the influence of knowledge/skill or judgment; second, to gain acceptance with the group. What are the results? Change, such as a new product; awareness or knowledge; different levels of motivation; a sense of affiliation within the group; and a new culture, one that exists within the group.

The best analogy is an athletic team. They are a dynamic culture of themselves. Think of a baseball team. One player is out of the lineup, and the team takes on a different dynamic and culture. For example, a veteran pitcher makes a difference in the confidence level of the other players. Various roles and experience—a player might bat better than field—can complement each other. The manager sets the positive climate, puts the players together like an organization manager, and turns the players loose to do what they do best. The relationship of combined experience, knowledge, and talent is what produces an effective team, a motivated team that works together to meet the goals and objectives.

Through Kurt Lewin's work we begin to see how groups interact and process. Lewin moved to the United States from Germany in the early '30s because of Hitler's rise to power. During World War II, Lewin was asked to teach people to change their eating habits because of food shortages. His research found that certain methods of group discussion and decision were superior to giving lectures and instructing for changing individuals' ideas and behavior. He found that informing people individually did not change their habits or attitudes about eating.

However, by discussing this in teams, members found out how others felt and began to express their viewpoints. Learning how to change eating habits was the result of the group process and interaction. Lewin examined the environment or atmosphere that takes place in a group: Knowles (1972) called this climate, Cattell (1956) called it syntality, Hall (1988), moving together.

Whatever the term, it referred to the environment of interaction. Today's organizations need teams to process information to achieve results: to do more with less time and money and fewer resources. Just like the baseball team, a business team has to establish goals, clarify roles, realize dependence and interdependence within the team, and know how to work together efficiently and effectively.

Combining individuals as resource teams creates a form in which shared energies create greater energy. It is like taking two 110 electrical lines to make a 220 line for an appliance such as an air conditioner. The two separate lines side by side cannot power the air conditioner; however, when combined in a single box to create a 220 line, the air conditioner works. It is this "combined energy" that gives the concept of team a significant place in organizations.

Teams produce better results than individuals through group interaction. This, in turn, can motivate individuals to have a greater impact, which may have greater input into the team process. The individuals become energized by the team interaction to achieve more. Now, metaphorically, a team member moves from being a 110 line to becoming energized like the 220 line powering the air conditioner.

But teams are not a utopia, nor are they always successful. Team members can violate the process and impede progress. Members can look for individual output rather than team concept. Uncontrollable elements (budgets, priorities, economy) also can deter team progress. Teams can work, but at what expense and at what outcome? The team concept can continue through combined energies of people who are committed to achieve agreed-upon goals and actions, enjoy the team process and group interaction, and produce rapport, trust, open sharing of talents, and the right results.

INTERACTIVE PROCESS

It is important for all members of a team to understand group interaction, individual behavior, and behavior within the team. The best predictor of future individual behavior is past behavior. So who are these people who make up this team? What do they bring to the table? Do they come to fight or listen; to examine, support, and build relationships; to direct or lead; to demonstrate knowledge or pontificate; to work together and achieve? The answer why each person comes to the team—perception developed by the people composing the team—will give you an idea of how the members will interact.

DYNAMICS OR INTERACTION WITHIN A TEAM

There are various traditional roles you can assume while being part of a team. Your role within the team depends on the topic, your expertise in that topic, and your level of confidence. There also is the level of individual and team motivation. Are you meeting to get a particular issue or action discussed? Did you meet to close or open the week's work? Do you value the meeting, and can decisions be made by the people in the team? What is the emotional involvement of the people in the team? Are they willing to work together?

The answers to these questions are the reasons for team interaction; yet very few people have the courage to openly begin a meeting by addressing these issues. By examining these points, an observer can see the level of trust, communication, and productivity, and gain insight into the organizational culture, as well as team dynamics.

Now let's examine the roles team members might assume. These are general descriptors of team member roles. Remember, team members may change roles at various times during the group process.

Leader—Listens and shares knowledge; expresses viewpoints; addresses questions; basically guides the team content discussion and facilitates the process.

Follower—Listens and expresses viewpoints to the team; supports, questions, or even challenges the leader.

Encourager—Helps achieve consensus; supports everyone to express their ideas.

Mediator—Clarifies different members' viewpoints; seeks a possible win-win solution; or expresses alternatives to the team discussion.

Sergeant—Sets and/or enforces the rules of team play; expresses organizational policies or procedures.

Comforter—Tries to relieve tension with anecdotes or humor; makes sure that no member is hurt.

Questioner—Asks relevant questions; wants to uncover and discuss the facts; encourages clarification of information.

Closer—Summarizes ideas and the progress of the team; checks to identify what action the team is willing to take.

Figure 1

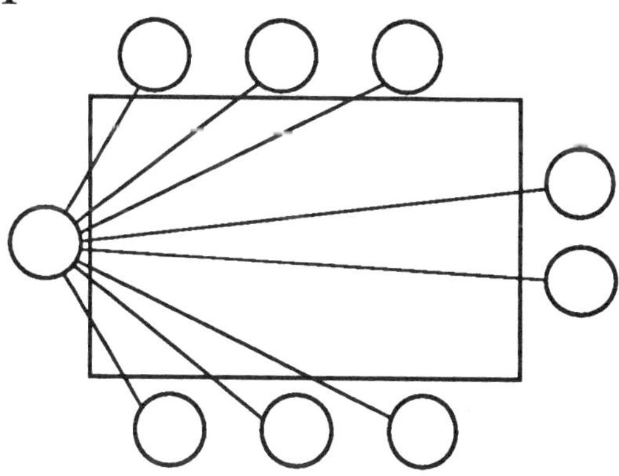

Leader is the focus.

Figure 2

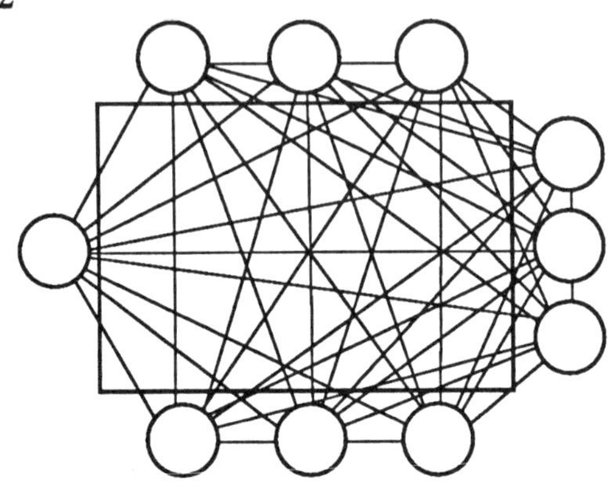

Group equal interaction.

Many times the dynamics within the group begin with the leader (Figure 1). The leader is either informing the team or facilitating the team process, which will generally progress to more of a group participation (Figure 2).

Moving from the more traditional method of examining team interaction, managers, supervisors, and professionals were asked to render a drawing of their concept of team dynamics and how they perceived themselves interacting. (These drawings show how people perceive team interaction. Even though crudely drawn, the realistic expression of team dynamics is captured.)

As you review the drawings, look for the person's expression of interaction (e.g., blocking, fear of risk taking, process orientation, etc.). Take a few minutes to think about what these people expressed about team dynamics.

Figure 3

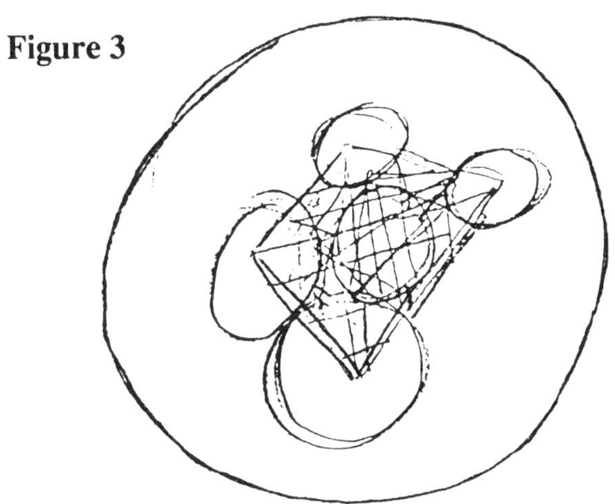

Indicates equal interaction, but look at the size of the circles and the enclosure of the large circle indicating structure.

Figure 4

The perceived traits of each member are shown: thinker, listener, one person "out to lunch," and a strong relationship between two people.

Figure 5

At first glance a happy team—but is there interaction?

Figure 6

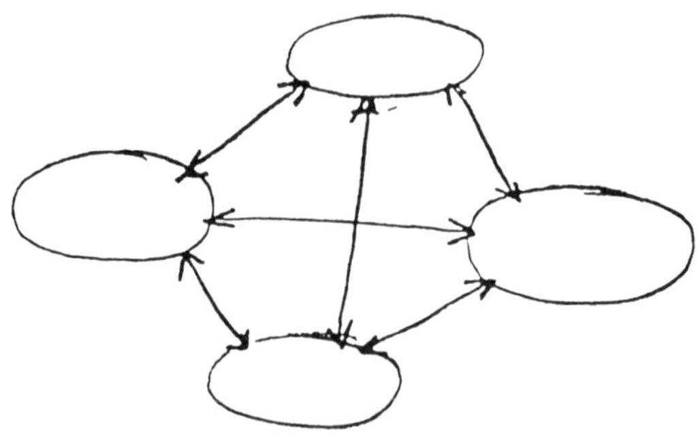

Structured, but equal, interaction.

Figure 7

*We/They: team interacting and being led by the leader,
but team isn't interacting with the leader.*

Figure 8

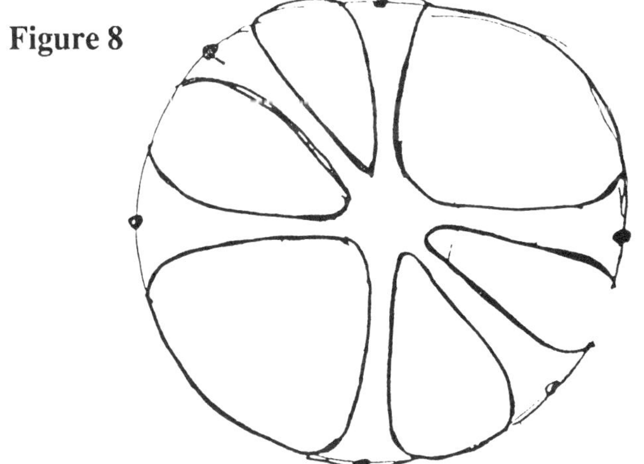

*Abstract, six people, dominance vary —but no interaction;
comfort level is probably high.*

Figure 9

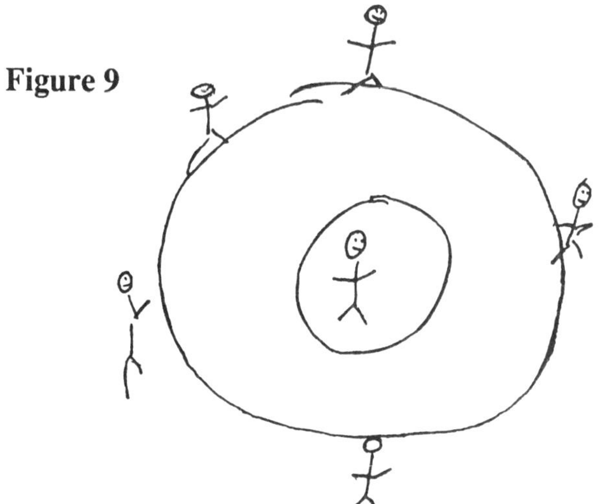

*Dominant leader with five individuals—
low level of interaction.*

Figure 10

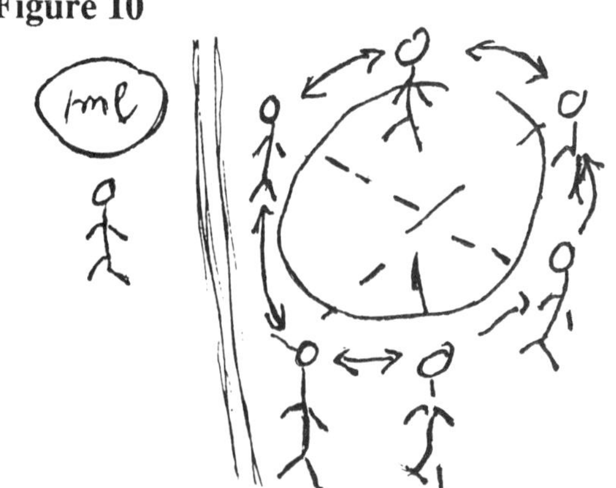

*The wall of separation for "me"—
leader and team working.*

Figure 11

The essence of a dominant leader who says,
"Do it my way!"

Figure 12

Change, development, growth—
unity in thinking.

In many respects these drawings say more than words could describe. They show the attitudes, frustrations, sharing, and development that people bring to a meeting.

We do not find the concept of self-directed teams in any of these drawings. The drawings depict traditional lines of structure and interaction. We need to move to a sense of more team and individual responsibility than the supervisor or manager having a strong sense of control. It is time to establish and fulfill the tight-loose relationship. Establish the direction and responsibility, then appropriately turn the employees loose to accomplish it. Based on individual abilities, everyone has a contribution to make, and that greatly increases through the dynamic interaction of the team. Self-directed teams can provide opportunities for responsibility that coincide with individual strengths and abilities.

6

SELF-DIRECTED TEAMS: LEADING FROM WITHIN

Self-directed teams (SDT) will be an integral way of doing business into the 21st century. There are a variety of functions a self-directed team can perform to carry out and fulfill organizational needs. *(See the 12 points and stages of development as discussed in Chapter Two.)*

Self-directed teams should: (1) clearly understand their purpose and importance to the organization; (2) know what the business objectives are, the expected results, and the needs and wants of key players and members of the team; and (3) establish the time frame or level of importance (i.e., long-term and critical aspects of day-to-day business as an ongoing process).

This type of team also needs to set a climate in which work can efficiently and effectively take place. Establishing a climate of openness, trust, and respect creates an environment for sharing. This allows conflict, yet focuses on agreement. It will help the team to become self-directed and independent, yet be responsible to meet organizational expectations. Self-directed also implies that the team will take action, be self-motivated to work together, and make appropriate decisions and recommendations.

Self-directed teams need to have a sense of inquiry to ensure that the right questions are asked, rather than coming up with random answers. Often members discuss what has occurred and then take action. In a sense, this puts the cart before the horse. Teams should measure *what* actions to take and know *why* they are taking them. Asking the right questions will define purpose, and determine what needs to be accomplished and the time frame for follow-up action.

For teams to be effective, there must be a sense of the *present* state, "What's happening now"; a clear vision of the *future desired* state; and a method of *transition* and *transformation* to attain. Today's "do more with less" approach to business has major corporations shifting to a more diverse portfolio. Their primary business is only part of their future diversity to arrive at their desired state. In the '90s, businesses will spend more time in transitional states than ever before. Self-directed teams will be critical to organizational success. They will help organizations deal with the needed flexibility to do business and to work in changing and transitional states.

The future of organizations depends on the leaders' ability to be flexible and innovative. Both flexibility and innovation need to occur to drive organizations to meet their future requirements. Leaders of organizations will need to develop long-term business plans that create clear vision (a direction to focus all organizational energies to work in sync), synergism, and symbioses (independent-dependent relationships). They will have to demonstrate commitment and openness, as well as share information that drives the organization. They should be the models from which all self-directed teams take their cue. Stagnant organizations will slowly whither and die.

This is what we have seen from Eastern Airlines, Gulf Oil, the automotive industry, Hills, Sears Department Stores, savings and loans, and hundreds of smaller companies. Flexibility and innovation have been lacking in most of these organizations.

But what about self-directed teams? They could be the saving grace of the future. The vehicle for organizations to make effective decisions, spread their message, and maintain their market share. Productively, they will pollinate the organization with ideas and carry the banner to success. These teams will be able to take quick action and adjust easily to change.

SDTs WORKING TOGETHER

The self-directed team is a major step for organizations committed to survive, through the survival of employees who are empowered. They focus on acquiring information to be applied in the future, maintaining the value system of the organization while dealing with change. They help to drive change yet maintain ongoing business. How will they do this?

The self-directed team can work at a comfortable pace and focus on accomplishing in the long term. The team acts as a micro, cross-cultural division working within the infrastructure to better the organization. Given the members of the team, the competency required to achieve within changing business situations, and time frames, the team often can achieve results in a more efficient and effective way.

Self-directed team members should:

1. Establish direction through team involvement. Understand purpose and results.

2. Establish priorities based on commitment.

3. Make decisions and initiate action based on commitment.

4. Follow up and assess action.

5. Define the team's boundaries or limitations. These limitations should be openly discussed and executive commitment understood.

What should *not* happen with any team is the coming together, meeting, and then seeing what occurs. By following these steps, energies are focused on particular goals; methods and strategies of action are discussed and implemented; and a timetable is used as a measuring post.

SDTs Initiating Action

Self-directed teams also need to take the initiative to examine the business environment. They must diagnose what needs to occur and formulate a prescription of action. In a sense, this moves some of the decision-making process to self-directed teams. Decisions can be made more quickly and effectively when they are made at the level of implementation.

An example of this is the research and design group working with manufacturing, sales and marketing, and purchasing to create a product and service within budget, which is available to customers on time. Think about this for a minute: more informed decisions being implemented quickly, effectively, and efficiently.

Empower the Team

Empowerment means to give others the freedom to make necessary decisions. Quality decisions are not made on the macro or "big picture" level alone—they are made on the micro or lowest possible level to meet the need of the people.

Empowering the self-directed team is what makes it work. Why? Because the self-directed team is free to make decisions and choices, and take responsibility on its own. The team is accountable to achieve its purpose and expected results.

Once business objectives are clear and agreed upon, then self-directed teams can be empowered by management, turned loose to function effectively but held accountable for their actions. This empowerment must be more than lip service. To succeed, there must be true commitment and follow-up.

Self-directed teams are an essential and necessary aspect of doing business and promoting the best process to share information and make correct decisions. Following are "The Cs to Success," which describe the elements needed to make a self-directed team work.

C aring	Respect for the members
C limate	Safe, encouraging environment
C ompany focus	Know business direction, objectives, and goals
C ustomer sensitivity	Know the customers' needs, wants, and desires

C ontinuous improvement	Strive for betterment
C ommitment	Support the team
C ourage	Take action and ask hard questions
C elebrate	Recognize efforts
C oncerns	Openly express ideas
C onsensus	Collect input from everyone and come to agreement

The Cs to Success provide a catchy method for making self-directed teams become a reality.

PROCESS VS. RESULTS

Working relationships should be built on substantive business issues (topics) of interest. The manner in which the facts (issues) are processed determines the outcome. It is not just facts but the discussion and interaction (synergism) that takes place in a business relationship that determines the results (actions) of the members.

Considering the expectations or desired business objectives, you need to plan ways to stimulate an open sharing of ideas among teammates. Create as safe an environment as possible given the people involved, the situation, and the desired results. You should begin by building trust and removing barriers. Be proactive in addressing difficult issues. Discuss issues of trust, process (how), and content/task (what) of business. An example of this is the CEO who feared losing his empire of 300 stores. He created fear and individually divided the Vice President because he feared conflict. The thing he feared most happened: no one worked together, and in a year, 100 stores were lost. He reluctantly sold the company. New management built teams, reliance, and open-ended communication and created a clear focus of direction. The company is again growing.

Establish daily business actions and methods of measurement; however, do not stifle creativity. Encourage open, honest, and respectful communication by modeling these communicative and interactive concepts. Help identify roles for all levels of employee involvement. Ensure that all employees (from vice president to maintenance worker) feel a part of the process by encouraging the sharing of experiences that could lead to future actions. Everyone on the team should know what action needs to be taken.

Back to our story of the company, now rebuilding the company. The VPs in charge of the company reorganized people to fit the new way of thinking and working. They created a vision, hope for them to recapture their position in the marketplace by turning the employees loose, empowering.

The Strategy/Results Interaction Model is found on the next page. Analyze the interaction between process and results.

INFLUENCING ACTION

Sharing ideas helps to keep the process ongoing, which focuses on meeting the desired results. To be an influencer you must continually be cognizant of the content and how it is processed (group interaction). At times, step back from the process to objectively analyze and measure what has been accomplished within a given period of time by writing the process and results you have observed.

As an influencer you must ensure that knowledge and task responsibilities are processed in a manner that is safe and productive for all levels of employees.

STRATEGY/RESULTS INTERACTION MODEL

High

Method	**Accomplish Results**
Interaction/Influence process; synergism—build trust; willing to listen; define task responsibilities; develop strategy. *"The How and What"*	Appropriate balance of method and vision; achieve results in the given time frame; combination of direction and results, influence process, and task responsibilities.
Accomplish Unwanted Results	**Vision**
Inappropriate balance of method and vision; redo work, deficiencies; accomplish after the fact or expected time period.	Focus on and know the desired results; develop actions toward results; ask the right questions; clearly focus on facts and issues; study the past, present, and future possibilities. *"The Direction"*

STRATEGY

Low ———— **DESIRED FUTURE RESULTS** ——— **High**

To accomplish your desired results you must clearly identify what you want. Identify the time period and method—influence process and task responsibilities—that will help you get what you want.

Positive Interaction

The purpose of identifying a business direction is to give clarity to achieve the desired outcome. Use supportive feedback (main/continue) and/or corrective feedback (develop alternatives) to adjust action throughout the interaction. A "positive outcome" does not mean that all the discussions are of a supporting nature; corrective feedback discussions can produce positive outcomes.

As part of the influence process, you should support all feedback through a willingness to listen. Supportive and corrective discussions are positive because both styles of interaction represent an open sharing of ideas. Focus on issues and guide your associates. Take follow-up action to ensure agreement and commitment to act.

Summary

The influence process that takes place is as important as the task responsibilities in achieving results. Involve all levels of employees as you collect their viewpoints. Create a safe environment and encourage and stimulate discussion through supportive and corrective feedback, note taking, and follow-up action. Create a focused direction and vision. Check the progress and establish a realistic time frame to accomplish what is needed.

1. Establish business outcome (results).
2. Involve all employees.
3. Develop strategy and vision.
4. Seek to understand all viewpoints.
5. Appropriately respond to meet needs of the organization, associates, and yourself.

CREATING A CHANGING MIND SET

Making the transition/transformation from the traditional workplace to teams requires more than logistical and organizational realignments. The people involved in team environments must be motivated to work with others as well as willing to sacrifice some of their personal goals for the good of the team. This thinking is contrary to what business has practiced since the first company was conceived. "You are born alone. You live alone. You die alone. But you work in teams."

Following are 10 axioms for changing the way you think about doing work.

1. Deal with the current situation on its own terms and develop alternatives. What do you want? What obstacles must be overcome?

2. Listen attentively without rebuttal—don't formulate answers while trying to listen. Understand others first.

3. Know how to apply information, rather than just "knowing."

4. Approach the future as a focused direction and beginning, not as a repetition or application of past events.

5. Use your *creative* processes (skills).

6. *Unconditionally* accept where you are and plan for the future. Do not put energy into or state, *"I/You should have . . . "* This builds guilt, embarrassment, and/or defense.

7.   As you plan, utilize your strengths. Establish a one-year plan through daily action, monthly planning, and reassessment.

8.   Realize that change involves risk taking.

9.   Do not be confined by parameters or rationalize your shortcomings.

10.   Have conviction and confidence to realize your vision; build credibility and trust; believe in yourself and act.

Members of the self-directed team should balance their thoughts to manage change.

LOGIC *(rationale)*	balanced with	**INTUITION**
PRECEDENCE *(innovation/ adaptation)*	balanced with	**CREATIVITY**
SECURITY/ **SAFETY**	balanced with	**RISK TAKING**
KNOWING	balanced with	**UNCERTAINTY**

"When the organization has a clear sense of its purpose, direction, and desired future state and when this image is widely shared, individuals are able to find their own roles both in the organization and in the larger society of which they are part."

Warren Bennis and Burt Nanus, 1985

ELEMENTS OF AN EFFECTIVE TEAM

An effective team should function as a unit to:

- Create Expectations
- Work Together
- Organize
- Share
- Build Relationships

Create Expectations—What does the team want to accomplish? This includes a mission statement, goals, and objectives. Identify the "whys" of the team, and all of the "hows" will fall into place. The accomplishments and/or results to be achieved should be measurable—know when and what the team has done.

Work Together—Set ground rules as to how the team will work together; create an effective and efficient manner to establish individual responsibilities—time frames to accomplish the responsibilities; give credit for jobs well done.

Establish a way to discuss issues and work through problems. Learn to negotiate, compromise, and develop alternatives.

Organize—Each member should have clearly defined roles and responsibilities. They should be encouraged to utilize their strengths to fulfill the team's objectives. Avoid overlapping jobs or responsibilities.

Share—Each team member must have a voice in the process; everyone should be encouraged to contribute. Remember to share what you feel safe and comfortable sharing—"What is politically wise?"

Build Relationships—All members need to develop an open, honest, trusting, and respectful relationship.

THE TEAM AS PART OF THE ORGANIZATION

Within a traditional organization there are three basic tiers: executive, management, and the workforce.

The *executive level* is where the decisions are made. Organizational structure and culture begin on this level with policies and procedures, business and succession plans, allocation of resources, and commitment of energy.

The *management level* carries out the desires and commitments of the executives. These people implement and, in some cases, mandate the organization to accept executive decisions. This middle level is a fulcrum between established direction and implementing that direction.

The *workforce level* conducts the leg work needed to sustain the organization. They are the front-line offensive in the business world.

The *self-directed team* can have various levels of input from different or diverse areas within the organization. Realistically, if an executive is involved in a self-directed team, the team process wanes because executives have a tendency to direct . . . and lower-level employees tend to remain passive because of fear of reprisal. Unfortunately, this scenario is all too true in today's organizations—yet the most creative and productive teams come from a mix of levels and departments.

Examine the Work Cycle Model.

THE WORK CYCLE

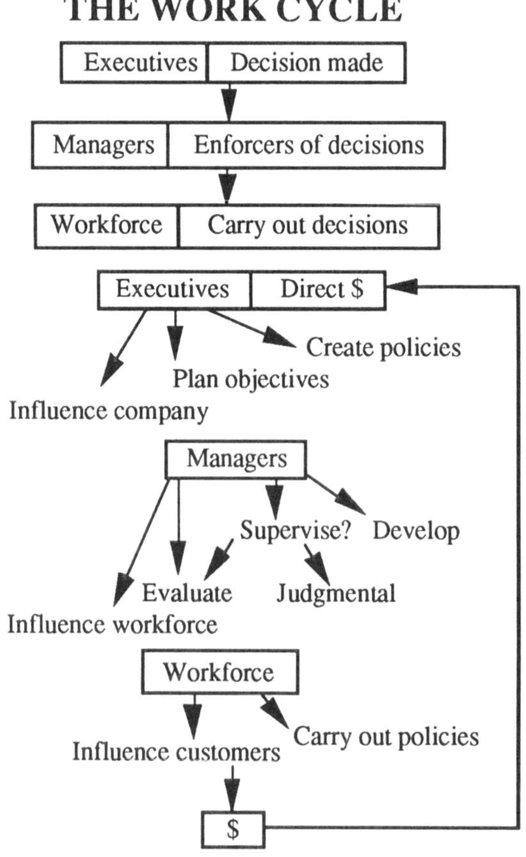

We need to build lines of communication in an upward motion so the workforce influence reaches management → to executives (to create policies, to have objectives through mutual input).

If self-directed teams are to be more than a fad, they need to become an integral part of day-to-day operations. Lines of positional authority need to be erased so that there can be an open sharing of information and debate to clarify direction and action. If the self-directed team is merely a continuation of authority by the highest-ranking person, it becomes a dictation rather than an exchange of information that will never reach its potential. Barriers such as authority and personal power might dictate and deter the progress of the organization.

Teams will become nothing more than the latest business fad. However, through all of this we all must have the confidence and courage to continue. To continue because change will occur no matter what we do. We have the option to let change direct our business lives or try to take initiative and make change work for us.

The challenge faces each person in the organization. Leaders and followers need to have ownership and involvement in their future, which can be accomplished through self-directed teams.

CONCEPT OF QUALITY

"All men dream; but not equally.

"Those who dream by night in the dusty recesses of their minds awake to find that it was vanity.

"But the dreamers of day are dangerous men, that they may act their dreams with open eyes to make it possible."

T. E. Lawrence

The achievement of quality is attained by asking the right questions rather than giving answers.

> Are there degrees of quality?
>
> What will cause you to achieve *total* quality?
>
> To achieve quality, are we using all available human resources right the first time?

To succeed, organizations need to do more than give lip service to quality. We must advocate quality efforts through processes that:

- measure improvements and remove deficiencies in products and services.

- encourage leadership, communication, meetings, interaction, and followership.

- ensure we do and say the right things.

- indicate we are "customer oriented" and market driven, and we define what makes our company unique.

- measure products and services at the appropriate level to meet and achieve business goals.

Quality is doing the right things right the first time. This implies that there are choices—*what things* and *at what time, with whom,* and *what risks need to be taken.*

How do we get employees on all levels to emotionally buy in to the process of productivity? We need people to lead, create a vision, and let everyone know the expected results. Employees must be encouraged to follow and be clearly told what is expected. The environment should allow risk taking and open communication, removing barriers that occur daily in every major corporation and firm.

We have to set clear measuring points by identifying the present state or condition and accepting where we are. Then, we can establish a future direction and the results that are needed and work backward establishing a plan. We can establish future direction and remain in a fluid transitional state to fill in the cracks. We need, metaphorically, to bolster our corporation like wet concrete, filling in the mold yet able to flow smoothly to another state. We need to benchmark and challenge ourselves to meet future productivity.

Present State—Unconditionally accept the present. There is nothing that can be done about the past, but we can learn and build on the past that caused the present.

Transformational State—We need to clearly understand the future direction and be flexible enough to meet changing business opportunities.

Future Desired State—Establish a vision, but help the organization to remain transitional and able to transform to a new direction. With change occurring quickly, we now have to think and be comfortable with instability rather than stability as the greatest factor for doing business.

Stable State—Somewhat predictable economy, production, workforce, government, management, leadership, stock market, competition, etc. We have to rethink stability in terms of flexibility and change with regard to our evolving work world.

> *"Quality is fitness for use. It's those products or service features that meet the needs of customers, provide customer satisfaction, and create sales. Quality also means freedom from deficiencies that create customer dissatisfaction."*
>
> J. Juran, 1989

Leaders need to clearly communicate and have the courage to confront and be held accountable and be willing to emerge as leaders. All employees need to have the conviction to a call to action. We find ourselves in the predicted times of change. We must hear that call to action.

COMMUNICATING A VISION OF QUALITY

It's one thing to talk about quality. It's another thing to do something about it. Statistical Process Control (SPC). Quality Circles (QC). Total Quality Process (TQP). We're all familiar with past and present quality buzzwords. The real answer to quality is not a fancy acronym or jargon term. In a word, it's teams. Through teams that live the philosophy of quality, the *"vision"* of hope is driven.

Effective teams are composed of several individuals who have various points of view but communicate a consistent message. Who have to tell the truth about what constitutes quality. In essence, communication is the glue that holds quality together.

> *"Many people have rich and deeply textured agendas, but without communication, nothing will be realized. The management of meaning, mastering of communication is inseparable from effective leadership."*

Warren Bennis and Burt Nanus, 1985

> *"High on the diagnostic checklist of corporate health is communication. The ease with which information flows downward, upward, and horizontally is often a major internal indicator of organizational effectiveness—who listens to whom may reveal the real as opposed to the apparent authority structure in the firm—and the proportion of people who consistently fail to get the message is frequently taken as a baseline for predicting efficiency."*

J. Hall, 1988

Quality Communication

- Identify the purpose for every meeting and phone conversation.
- Delivery—effectively deal with time, changes, materials, informing others, setting priorities.
- Follow up to measure what was accomplished.
- Meeting—start and finish on time.
- Clarify phone calls the first time.

Process

- Gain commitment.
- People accountable—placing demand.
- Listen—respond.
- Time/cost/value—ration/fitness of your communication.

People Side of Quality Communication

- Care, commitment, communication.
- Continuous focus on customer.
- Challenge, courage, celebration.
- Concern.

Are we advocates for quality—saying and discussing the right things with commitment written in water? Or, are we committed to the courses of quality on the interactive scale? Do we legitimize the quality process and influence through the right action? How you answered these questions will determine where your organization stands and how much you can influence change.

Implementing Quality Through Influence

Here are some guidelines for influencing quality change efforts:

- Establish direction to focus energy and clarify options.
- Establish a clear plan of action and the benefits of accomplishment.
- Develop alternatives. Be flexible.
- Listen effectively—seek to understand others first—understand needs, then respond to the needs—yours and theirs.
- Share your ideas, power, authority, prestige, influence—involve everyone.
- Listen and respond openly—be willing to be influenced.
- Understand conflict and gain agreement.
- Establish a safe environment in which to discuss change.
- Build rapport, trust, and respect.
- Gain commitment to achieve quality.

Organizations need to establish direction and give employees (teams) the opportunity to make an impact. High control and dictation do not lend themselves to today's constantly changing work environments. Innovation is ongoing, as is continual improvement, which means continual change. Quality improvements will increase morale, productivity, and financial capacity, which support individual performance. This leads to self-motivated employees, self-directed teams, and an overall commitment to achieve. Turn the workforce loose to do what they do best—their jobs.

CAUSES FOR CHANGE

Here are some common reasons for change: new technology, competition, economy, need, want, desire, a recognition of other people, equipment, products, service or economics changing; realize a better approach; concept of improvement supported by present technology.

Key issues for implementing the change process are similar to those for implementing the influence process.

1. Define and prioritize what you want to accomplish.

2. Develop a process strategy and a method of measurement to recognize achievement.

3. Identify concepts of change and its effects on the organization and target group(s).

4. Evaluate the commitment of the sponsors and their wherewithal and ability to succeed.

5. Have the courage to continue.

Think of yourself as an ice cube that has melted at room temperature. In that liquid state you mold and reshape easily. Today we must remain liquid and in the transformational state to meet the challenges of the future. If a team became liquid, the energy would be combined and able to easily adapt.

CHANGE PROCESS

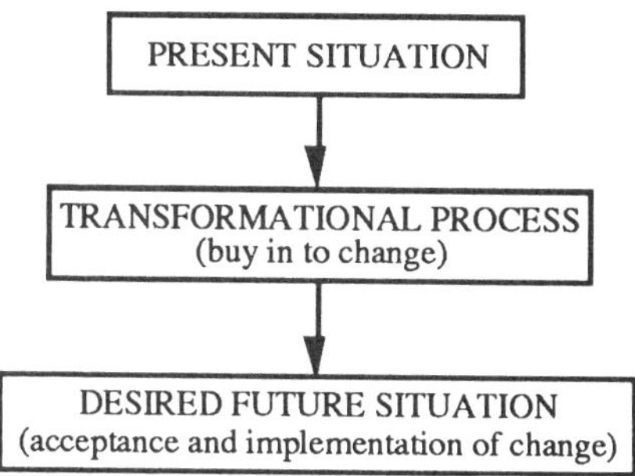

Background

Analyze the present situation—what led up to this situation—what is occurring now—what will be the outcome without change—what will be the outcome with change, improvement, fewer deficiencies, addressing or emphasis on business issues.

Reason to Change

Identify needs, wants, and desires that are the causes for change. Why should you make a change? This means that the present thinking has to be replaced with future thinking. There has to be an emotional buy-in, a change in attitude, a replacing of a mind set.

Comparison

Compare the enhanced future state to your present state. Now, imagine a period of transition, or that the organization will remain in the transformational state continually reshaping to meet new and future demands, remain flexible. Which do you prefer?

Trade-Offs

Future goals often require the present to change. You must develop alternatives for the process and how you approach the work to be done. Innovative and creative thinkers develop alternatives. They continually strive for flexibility and weigh the pros and cons of their actions.

SUMMARY

The change process that takes place is as important as the task responsibilities in achieving results. Involve all levels of employees and collect their viewpoints. Create a safe environment and encourage and stimulate discussion through supportive and corrective feedback, note taking, and follow-up action. Create a focused direction and vision. *Check the progress* and establish a realistic time frame to accomplish what is needed.

1. Establish business outcome (results).

2. Involve all employees.

3. Develop strategy and vision.

4. Seek to understand all viewpoints.

5. Appropriately respond to meet needs of the organization, associates, and yourself.

"Today we need to enhance and improve our products and services to meet the challenges of the future."

"We can no longer rest on laurels. We must be flexible and constantly change to meet and exceed customer need and organizational value. To accomplish this we must be willing to measure the process."

"We need to create an equality among all employees so each individual feels involved and committed to organizational achievement."

"Leaders can no longer solely rely on authority to lead, they must be influencers."

7

MYTHS OF TEAM BUILDING

Every group will not become a team! There are leaders of teams of workers, or groups who have little desire, who resist becoming a team. Why? Traditions, standards, culture, way of business history are some of the main reasons. The team actually is a subgroup or culture, which promotes acceptance to function as individuals—not as a team. Resistance, avoidance, or the sense of belonging are to be separate from this "counter culture," not one of becoming a corporate or business team. Recently, this author worked with a group of first-line supervisors who didn't work together as a team, nor did their hourly employees want to work as a team. Comments such as: "Tell me what to do"; "I'm not paid to think"; and "I'll work my shift—that's it" were commonplace. Could this group of individuals come together as a team? This poses an interesting question. These individuals could come together as a team if they changed the way they perceived themselves in the workplace. Is teamwork an awareness? A perception? A willingness that leads to the team concept? Yes!

If the purpose is clear—if the team has established a focused direction and its members agree on action— and the members are open enough to express themselves and involve themselves in input (suggestions), then yes, a team can develop.

Teamwork is nurtured by recognizing and rewarding quality work. A leader can pull together a group to become a team. However, two factors—motivation and desire to become a team—are essential. This might occur in particular times of crisis. A crisis fosters cooperation. The army did a study during the Vietnam War about racism. A high degree of cooperation was exhibited by two soldiers in a foxhole fighting the enemy. While one soldier fed the bullets, the other fired the machine gun. Occasionally, leaders perpetuate crises because they mistakenly mask real teamwork by putting employees in a "business foxhole." Therefore, employees feel they have to perceive themselves as a team and are willing to become a team.

Some unions and hourly workers avoid becoming members of the business team because they believe that to do so goes against the subculture and affiliation of the rank and file. This is not a pro or con statement about hourly or union employees, rather an observation of reality after working with many organizations.

PROBLEMS

The main problems are a *"we-they"* syndrome, low trust, and communication that is directed solely at getting results. It takes time and effort to build rapport, and a realization that all employees need to be held accountable for meeting the organization's needs and business goals. The point of this is that the *"we-they"* syndrome is a very individualized concept. Teamwork takes time, and once developed into "all of us," it becomes a source of pride for each member.

Through a suggestion system, Toyota has involved its employees and, in a sense, created ownership into the Toyota system. How? The manager recognizes employees' suggestions and responds within 24 hours after receiving the suggestion. There is recognition and a reward for people making a suggestion. Employees/working associates are rewarded with membership into the Gold, Silver and Bronze Clubs. Furthermore, 96% of the employees' suggestions were implemented reflecting management's commitment through action. Unfortunately, communication often is the sole reason many programs and suggestions die. Supervisors point fingers at employees; managers point fingers at supervisors. Vice presidents dictate, but no one clearly communicates because of the lack of shared information. Lower-level employees gain information through the grapevine. We give lip service to unity—words, words, and more words—when what is needed is *action*. These days of change are times of risk taking. Employees and managers need to address issues proactively. It is easy to complain and wait. Playing it safe in business today is, in effect, a short-term comfort and long-term disaster. Slow action and reaction will not drive the team concept or quality.

Quick fixes and slick approaches will not provide long-term results to group commitment. Unified achievement should be the goal for the future. All employees should have a sense of wanting to achieve. Many employees are like the batter who goes to home plate just wanting to reach first base. The batter thinks, "I hope the pitcher throws me four balls." Business today requires people who want to hit the ball—a line drive up the middle—and can be hard-hitting, consistent batters.

ADDRESSING THE TEAM-BUILDING PROBLEM

We need to make sure that information is overshared today. How can we ask employees to trust our decisions without demonstrating we trust them. We communicate through actions and words. For effective communication, our actions must equal what we say. We need to develop a Say=Do equation throughout the business world. Trust is the adhesive that holds teams, divisions, and corporations together. It might be easier when everyone knows the competition and has a clear understanding of the business objectives.

Trust, clear communication of business objectives, a plan of action, the flexibility to adapt, demonstrating openness, and the sharing of information are the ingredients for success. All levels of employees must be held accountable and committed to achieve these objectives. Information cannot get stuck in the middle or miscommunicated. Leaders have to lead, making sure that trust, communication, action, and flexibility are driven to all levels of the social culture of their organizations. Leaders have to hear a call to arms. They must ensure that the sense of organizational purpose is clearly driven throughout the organization, and each employee needs to know that his or her tasks and responsibilities support that purpose.

Some people might read this and say, "More fluff." Successful communication—carefully chosen words and actions by the speaker, proactive listening and follow-up actions by the listener—is a battle. It takes hard work to initiate action and move an organization, and the only way this can occur is to have everyone pulling in the same direction, working toward the organization's mission. All employees should know the benefits of working together. We have to go back in history, when employees had pride in what they did and felt a sense of accomplishment. Today, money is what employees look for. It seems that money has replaced organizational pride. Is organizational pride still alive?

At some point, employees have to revert to a level of accomplishment and pride in themselves and the work they do regardless of the service provided. Employees should have a sense of what it is they are accomplishing to achieve the organizational purpose. How do they do it? Through accountability, making sure there is equity, and confronting managers, supervisors, and employees who block or don't use the system. Time and money are wasted because of ineptness, a feeling of "business as usual," avoidance, or because the current system is easier.

The time-cost ratio needs to be examined, and every employee needs to tie into the organizational purpose in a realistic, business, social, and humane way. We need to build employee involvement and recognize and reward what the organization wants to become. We have to feel comfortable with change because through change comes improvement. By continually addressing business issues proactively and maintaining quality, organizations today will have the necessary flexibility to change.

This author has collected information from hundreds of supervisors and managers on the strengths and problems of businesses today, and possible solutions. The following list summarizes these strengths, problems, and solutions.

Strengths	**Problems**
Quality process	Lack of career advancement
Global concepts	Lack of innovation
Technology	Office politics
Workforce	Reward "yes" people
Leaders' commitment	Disloyalty
Financial stability	Lack of strong upper management
	Instability
	Not risk takers
	Lack of communication/business direction
	Follow-up
	Common sense

Solutions

- Communicate—share information.
- Question—ask the right questions and stop throwing out answers.
- Be visible.
- Leaders need to talk with all levels of employees daily and weekly.

- Stay accountable to run meetings effectively on all levels.

- Follow up—Say=Do.

- Leaders and employees need to be enthusiastic and realistic.

- Define responsibilities for all levels of employees.

- Set priorities.

- Develop an effective feedback system that is realistic and truthful, and rewards honesty.

- Explain when change occurs—communicate flexibility.

- Take risks—being in business is a risk itself.

- Don't forget why you are in business in the first place.

- Drive involvement throughout the organization "suggestion system."

- Help each employee to realize the contribution he or she makes in addressing the organizational purpose.

By accomplishing these points, you can start addressing the causes of quality. These solutions are not easy to achieve, but common sense says they need to be addressed. Maintaining an organization is like maintaining a body. The organization must undergo exercise, watch its diet, deal with cuts and bruises, buy new apparel when the old clothing (facade) is worn out, adapt to new situations, take the appropriate medicine when necessary, socialize, create a marriage, love, hate, rejoice over birth and grieve death, balance the mental health, and know when to rejoice, celebrate, and rest, all to maintain a long, healthy life.

Employees must realize that they did not inherit the organization's reins from previous leaders who were committed to the concepts and missions of the past. It is the future portals that an organization must go through. Today's leaders borrow the reins of leadership from the future leaders of the organization.

This is nothing new. The great corporate founders and leaders—Carnegie, Westinghouse, Sloan, and Edison—built a vision of the future. Contemporary leaders with the future in mind need to manage an improvement process through people involvement, thereby creating an organizational ownership for each employee that is appropriate for his or her level of commitment. We can't let the "analysis of paralysis" poison our thoughts to drive toward the future. Looking toward the future will make the vision of opportunities clearer through a *customer*-driven product/process/ service and help achieve the organization's goal— success—given the business climate and competition.

How do we achieve success? By asking the right questions, working toward the right answers, and implementing and driving those answers to achieve the right results for today, with an eye on the future.

Long-term plans—the organization's future—can be established and met if leaders:

- Drive the organization to meet customer/employee satisfaction.

- Use all available resources in the organization, especially the suggestions of employees who have their hands on the product and service.

- Promote and reinforce individual learning and growth to ensure organizational learning.

- Build an open, honest, respectful, and trusting environment; Say=Do.   Communicate words through actions.

- Support innovation through flexible adaptation to customer/organizational needs, wants, and desires.

- Maintain a level of excellence, internally benchmark to show continual improvement.

- Create a sense of equality and consistency throughout the organization.

- Overshare information from the top level to the lowest level, recognizing all employee contributions.

- Create a climate that rewards excellence rather than establishes minimum parameters to avoid punishment.

- Plan for the future; establish a vision, business objectives, and a strategy to achieve success.

These points are a realistic, commonsense approach to helping all levels of employees feel part of the organization and work toward its success. The only limits of creativity in achieving success are locked in our minds. Bringing out the leader potential in each of us is a way to drive creativity in the organization. Two types of skills are necessary to attain this potential: people skills and task skills, which are outlined below.

People Skills

Clarity of
  communication/Listening

Rapport	Conflict/Resistance
Openness	Discipline
Motivation	Trust
Self-esteem	Training/Learning feedback

Task Skills

Employee/
  Management satisfaction

Results	Time management
Problem solving	Customer satisfaction
Technical expertise	Work assignments
Planning	Accountability

The style of leadership that we bring to the job is a combination of people and task skills. This is the reality of doing what we do best, bringing together the team, using the appropriate balance, given the attitudes and climate of the workplace. It is the attitudes of the individual employees and the atmosphere or climate in which they work that also can be the downfall of teamwork. Every group will not necessarily become a team. It is not an automatic. But if you are attentive to the issues of the individual employees, there can be growth and development from the status quo.

To begin addressing team-building issues and finding out if a group can come together as a team, examination of four areas is necessary:

- Brainstorming/Problem solving

- Analyzing a discussion

- Resistance

- Effective listening

Effective, successful teams work at all four of these areas. Gaps in any or all four would require the leader to question whether the group of employees can and/or ever will become a team.

BRAINSTORMING/PROBLEM SOLVING

Background

Alex F. Osborne (1952) originated the idea of brainstorming or creative problem solving, the generating of ideas. He emphasized deferred judgment about any idea, stating that the mind could not produce ideas and judge or evaluate them at the same time. Brainstorming generates ideas, possibilities, or alternate courses of action. By moving from a specific problem to general ideas about that problem, the person expands their thinking on the original, specific problem. The point is to generate as many ideas as possible (wild ideas), use one idea as a take-off point for generating more ideas, and clarify items to expand the thinking about the original, specific point. Studies have shown that some of the best ideas come later on in the brainstorming process. This explanation will examine ways to brainstorm and ask you to become actively involved in the problem-solving process.

Expected Results

- That each participant will actively participate in the problem-solving groups.

- That each participant will understand problem solving and use this technique, when appropriate, back in the workplace.

- That each participant will learn from each other and gain insight into the corporation through the brainstorming exercises.

Problem solving could be a means through which you could better understand or expand your thinking about personal as well as business concerns. There are two basic assumptions about brainstorming/problem solving:

1. Suspending judgment about an idea increases productivity and promotes the generation of ideas.

2. Because various ideas are generated, quantity, in this case, promotes quality—that is, quality ideas can be chosen from the quantity of ideas.

Effective brainstorming builds a sense of trust, openness, honesty, respect, a willingness to accept, listen, share ideas, and supports efforts to achieve a specific goal.

Brainstorming

Brainstorming is the gathering of help from others to address a situation or question to which you do not have an answer. This should involve every appropriate person. Have each person give one or more ideas. Any concept that relates to the problem is a relevant response. Continue this process until all possible responses have been exhausted. Figure 1 shows a model of generating and developing ideas through the metaphor of ice cream cones.

PROBLEM SOLVING MODEL

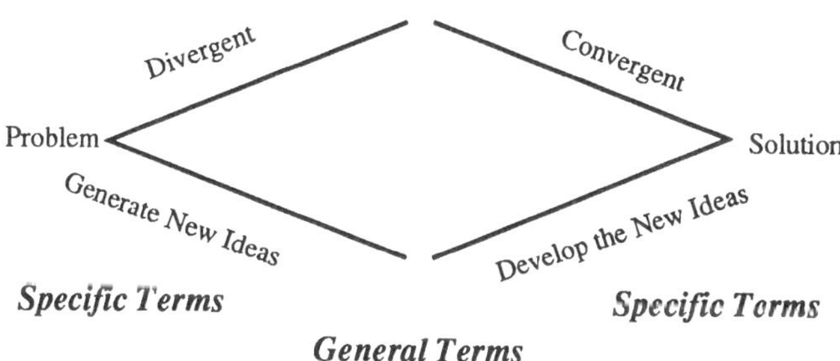

Figure 1

1. Focus on one idea (specific). Have a discussion.

2. Put that problem on a visual (paper, blackboard) and draw a circle around it. Collect responses about the problem. List any idea even remotely related to the problem (divergent).

3. As an example, we will brainstorm "communication." List every idea about communication around the circle as illustrated in Figure 2.

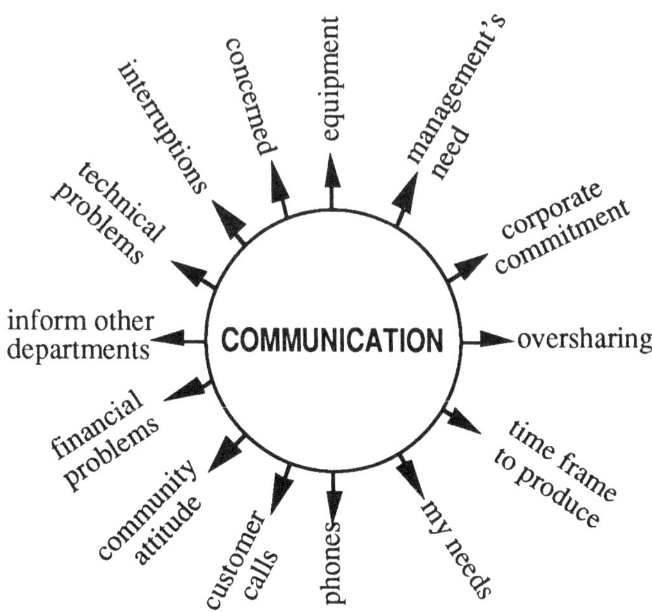

Figure 2

4.   After the ideas are written, begin to prioritize by focusing on specific areas, listing the ideas that are pertinent to the discussion. Divide the list into two areas: (a) high priorities, and (b) low priorities. From the general, you are becoming specific (convergent). Develop alternatives to the problems. Developing alternatives is a creative way to effect change.

Example:

High Priorities:	**Low Priorities**:
inform other departments	interruptions
technical problems	my needs
corporate commitment	phones
oversharing	financial problems

Communication—two high priorities:

> (1) inform other departments
>
> (2) technical problems

5. Identify your concerns about the problem and solicit the concerns of others about the problem.

Example:

Communication   choose one of the priorities and develop a solution

(1) inform other departments

- contact John from . . .
- hold interdepartmental meetings
- inform upper management
- notify . . .
- communicate technical problems

6. Address ways to solve the problem or provide the next step toward a solution. Ask how you might act or implement your problem-solving solution. Follow up and let all involved know what action is taken.

Summary

1. Identify the problem.

2. Generate all possible ideas.

3. Create a connection between the specific problem and your ideas to create a solution.

4. Plan a strategy, act and implement your strategy, collect feedback, assess the strategy, and make any necessary changes.

REFLECTION MODEL

Utilizing the Reflection Model (Figure 3) below will help to create an awareness of where you are and where you want to go (mentally, philosophically, and physically) given your wants, needs, desires, and motivation. Develop a plan to act. This is essential when dealing with change of any kind. Be proactive. Initiate action rather than being reactive or passive. Plan to achieve your potential on an ongoing basis.

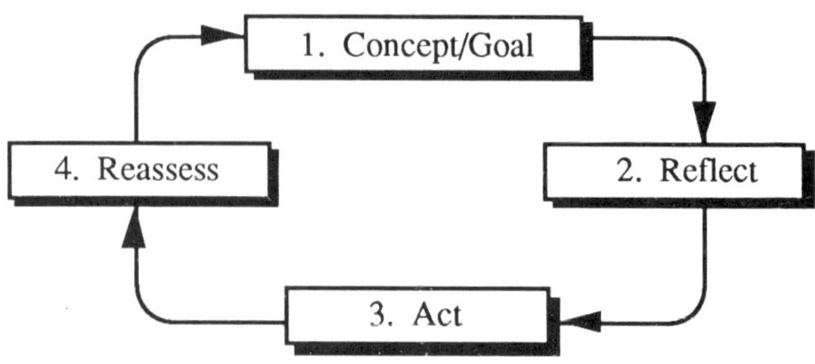

Figure 3

1. **Concept/Goal**—The first step in determining how you'll tackle an element in the workplace is to develop a goal. Any analysis requires collecting data. Collect data relevant to cause—not just what is occurring. Develop a realistic plan of action.

2. **Reflect**—Now is the time to brainstorm ideas. Don't limit yourself. Create strategies and explore methods for implementing your ideas.

3. **Act**—Implement your ideas of a strategy/ methodology within a specific, realistic time frame. Be patient and keep momentum once you begin.

4. **Reassess**—Because no process is 100 percent foolproof, you'll want to periodically assess your progress. This review actually occurs at each step in the process.

    a. recognizing strengths and problems (utilize your strengths)

    b. assessing risks

    c. collecting unbiased information

    d. having the courage to continue

Reflect on a personal goal and write your comments under each point (this will not have to be shared):

Personal Goal:

____

____

____

Reflect:

____

____

____

Act:

____

____

____

Reassess:

____

____

____

FOLLOW-UP FOR BRAINSTORMING

Acknowledge what others say, not just what you think they should say, or want them to say. Listen to what is said, not just what you want to hear.

THE 3 A'S

Acquire

1. Find the right person with the data.

2. Collect unbiased data by asking questions.

3. Clarify what was said by paraphrasing.

Acknowledge

1. Identify problems and clearly state them.

2. Use brainstorming.

3. Have others discuss possible solutions and summarize.

Act

1. Devise a sequential action plan (Step 1, Step 2, etc.).

2. Develop a realistic time frame to carry out and complete the action plan.

3. Create guidelines for reassessment of the action plan.

ANALYZING A DISCUSSION

People interact differently because of the role each person assumes in a discussion. The more you are aware of the roles of the people who are interacting, the better you are able to respond to their and your needs.

People may assume any one of these different styles of interaction during a discussion. As a presenter/listener, you should utilize all of the styles of interaction listed below and on the next page, except for attacking.

Pausing   silence; words are interwoven on a background of silence; a pause can emphasize and clarify.

Explaining   describe something; tell; disseminate information.

Paraphrasing   reiterate; restate; clarify; mirror the words that were stated.

Questioning   ask questions; get a better understanding.

Listening   collect, interpret, and give meaning to information.

Feeling   express an effective opinion: "I feel that . . ."; share information.

Reinforcing   support: "I agree with that because ..."

Relating   tell a story; relate an experience.

Challenging	disagree intellectually; discuss an argumentative point.

Humoring	break the ice; joke.

Interjecting	politely interrupt: "Excuse me, but . . ."; touch the arm of the speaker; break eye contact.

Attacking	personal; verbal assault on a person with little regard for facts.

Question: Who controls a discussion—the speaker, the listener, or both? Why?

How to Address Questions

Listen without rebuttal. Show interest by making eye contact, nodding your head indicating acceptance of what the person says; then:

Listen to how the question is asked.

1. "Do you see what I mean about . . . ?" (visually)

2. "Doesn't that say something about how . . . ?" (aurally)

3. "Don't you feel that . . . ?" (emotionally)

Address the questions in the same mode.

1. "I see. . . . "; "I imagine. . . . "; "I look. . . . "; "In my mind's eye. . . . "; "My viewpoint is. . . ." (visually)

2. "I hear that. . . . "; "I'll tell you. . . . "; "I am attuned to. . . . "; "Let me reiterate. . . . "; "In response to. . . ." (aurally)

3. "I feel. . . . . "; "My gut level feeling is. . . . "; "Emotionally I agree. . . . "; "You can reach out to. . . ." (emotionally)

Listen to the terms of the questions.

1. Were they specific or general?

2. Specific (analytical) terms should be addressed with analytical, detailed, or data-supported answers. Paraphrase agreement.

3. General (big picture, global) terms could be addressed in speculative, feeling, suggestive, all-encompassing terms. Paraphrase agreement.

Be concise. If someone asks how you are, do not give a minute-by-minute update. Answer the questions in an appropriate, succinct manner that meets the listener's needs.

If you are confused or need to have a point clarified, interject or ask a question. Do not let the discussion go on. The other party assumes that there is mutual understanding if the discussion continues without interruption.

When someone asks a question for which you do not readily have an answer:

1. Listen attentively (make eye contact, acknowledge).

2. Ask a question in return. This will give you more time to think of an appropriate response.

Examples:

- Why do you ask that?

- That is a very interesting thought; could you expand upon your idea?

- What do you think the ramifications of that would be?

- How do you think that could be accomplished?

If you do not know an answer to a question:

1. State that you do not know.

2. Emphasize the resources you have available for finding the answer (research, data, personnel, networking system, etc.).

3. Let the questioner know that you will follow up and get back to him/her.

4. Set a time frame for the follow-up.

Listening is more important than responding. Answers need to be focused according to the question.

RESISTANCE

"The ability to avoid getting what you don't want from yourself, others, and the environment."

H. B. Karp, 1985

- Resistance to change lies in our perceived successes . . . because we have been successful, we do not want to change.

- Resistance to change can be due to:

  —a feeling of familiarity.

  —a feeling of safety and security.

  —a feeling of "I can" that has been reinforced by tradition, standards, and competitors.

- All new concepts eventually become outdated—continual improvement means change.

- Develop alternatives—adaptations—innovations—creativity—problem solving to meet future needs.

	I Want	**I Don't Want**
I Get	Power	Victim
I Don't Get	Loser	Resistance

H. B. Karp, 1985

Did you realize that power and resistance are closely aligned? Passive-Resistance, if I have no organizational or positional power, then I can resist to get what I want. Realize that you fall into various quadrants based on the situation.

How do you deal with resistance?

1. Listen—honestly hear what people say.

2. Show empathy, concern—understanding.

3. Acknowledge, paraphrase—what the person states or says.

4. Respectfully respond now that you understand the resistance.

EFFECTIVE LISTENING

Listening, the willingness to accept what someone says, is an honest approach toward building a relationship or team rapport with others. By listening, you give a sense of recognition and worth to someone. Look at the person speaking, make eye contact, show interest. This doesn't indicate agreement or disagreement; it shows concern.

Effective listening is part of effective communication. One person has to effectively present information, and one person has to effectively listen to the information given. Listen means you heard or read what and how it was said, and there is a decision about action. To effectively collect information, one must listen and adapt to the presentment style of the speaker. Everyone has a different style of speaking and listening. People are greatly influenced by *what* is said, *how* it is said, *who* says it, and *when*, *where*, and *why* it is said.

Various influencing factors alter the acceptance to what is said. These factors also affect the perception and interpretation of what is said. The different communication styles and behaviors are developed through education, life experience, and the expectations of the work environment. There are many different ways to effectively speak and listen. The people involved in the communication, the situation, and the environment greatly influence the effectiveness of communication. Depending on the given circumstance or environment, a listening style could plausibly be appropriate (saying "uh ha," nodding your head, hand movements, etc.), and the various communication styles and behaviors of bold, expressive, sympathetic, technical, passive, assertive, open, and concealed aggressive.

Listening and speaking are of equal importance in effective communication. The purpose of communication is to *disseminate, share,* and *collect information.* The effective listener unbiasly collects information in the manner it is presented. The information should be interpreted first on the speaker's terms, and then the listener's. The main resultant of effective communication is the mutual understanding of the speaker's and listener's terms. Mutual understanding implies that the communication is interpreted on a mutual level of comprehension. Presenter and listener understand it in the same manner. The purpose of effectively speaking and listening is to establish a mutual result from the interaction, creating partners (speaker/listener) in communication.

Simply stated, the listener needs to be flexible enough to use the same "communication system" as the speaker to create a mutual understanding.

How do you relate to the various communication styles and behaviors as a listener? The basic premise is that you, as a listener, *take in the information without rebuttal.* You then interpret what is said—compare, clarify, evaluate, and create a mental perception to deal with the information. The best way to do this is to concentrate on what is said rather than immediately thinking of a response. Pausing does not imply agreement or disagreement. Pausing or reflecting on what and how it was said gives you time to mentally digest and begin to apply, analyze, synthesize, evaluate, receive, and respond to the information. To be a better, active listener focuses you on what and how it is said rather than to immediately respond.

"No matter how good the communication, if no one listens, all is lost. The best communication forces you to listen."

Max DePree
Leadership Is an Art, 1989, p. 102

WHEN DON'T YOU LISTEN EFFECTIVELY?

List circumstances in which you don't listen effectively.

____

____

____

____

____

Why Don't People Listen?

- time, time, time
- same old stuff
- a complaint
- fed up—tired
- no interest
- something else to do
- lack of trust—don't like the speaker
- waste of time—better things to do
- disagree—nothing in this for me
- don't value the information
- this is not true

So Then—Why Do They Listen?

WAYS TO INFLUENCE THE LISTENER

The right: people, information, time, place, circumstance

- Know the goal—what is to be accomplished.
- Know the listener.
- Know your communication style and behavior.
- Express the benefits for the listener: "What this means for you is. . . ." Relate business examples, stories.
- Show competence and confidence.

- Be open, honest, respectful, trusting, and straightforward.

- Establish the right time and place to meet for someone to listen.

- Measure the results.

List the *benefits from effectively listening*. For example: update, learn the right action to take, diffuse anger, build rapport and trust, gain more knowledge.

____

____

____

____

____

____

SUMMARY

Acknowledge and know the type of people who compose the team and develop an approach to address team-building issues. Every group has the potential of becoming a productive team; however, a group could turn into a gang. Don't try to make people into something they might not want. Be realistic and practical in your thoughts about teamwork and development.

8

REALIZING CHANGE

Looking back on critical periods of this century—1910-18, 1929-39, 1940-45—and how different people were—there was a sense of unity through crises. People were polite and biased, with the common cause of industrial development, war, and Depression to bring them together. As we view the '60s, '70s, and '80s, we have a sense of "what's in it for me." Common cause has seemed to vanish.

What's wrong with our businesses? Why do we promote speed over quality? What happened to a common cause?

To explain this phenomenon, picture a never-ending train ride in which you are placed at birth. As you age, you can look to the left and right to clearly see what is occurring. You can look back to see where you've been. You look ahead, but you're uncertain as to direction. Many of us today (baby boomers) didn't experience World War I, the Depression, World War II, and the Korean War, but our "trains" covered those tracks. Other cultural trains covered different tracks. We can't forget the ride we have taken. Yet we want to enjoy the experience we are having now without the uncertainty and doubt of what will happen next.

As the years go by, the train seems to pick up speed. Change occurs so fast that we cannot seem to grab onto the safety and security of knowing what is going to occur. We can lament the past, complain about the present, and worry about the future, but what we need is confidence in ourselves to make the right decisions without the knowledge of what the future will bring.

We have to become comfortable, flexible, and capable of successfully dealing with change faster than at any other time in history. And yet, we know that the uncertainty of change and the competition of the future are creating a stressful and anxiety-filled work environment.

INDIVIDUAL DEVELOPMENT

The ability to change is an important part of the business environment. Every day people are forced to adapt to circumstance. Some people do this better than others because of organizational and interpersonal skills. Their adaptation to circumstance could be as minor as handling a telephone interruption or as major as assuming new job responsibilities.

As people learn to use their knowledge at home and work, they should reflect upon how and why they acquired this knowledge. New forms of technologies have forced many people to change and adapt their skills. How many people design organizational development plans, create strategies to develop interpersonal skills, and have an awareness of new theories in their fields of interest?

Often people become complacent because they have been performing the same type of job responsibilities for a long period of time. Changes are not seen as necessary because job performance is rated as satisfactory. Yet change could be refreshing and a motivation for internal growth.

Change is an acquisition of knowledge and a method of thought, not the acquisition of instruments like the computer. Change often requires creative thinking. Begin to use your creative abilities and dream of new frontiers. Practice creativity while speaking and thinking about how to solve a problem or establish expectations.

Creativity can be analyzed as two concepts: adaptation and innovation. Adaptation is the improvement of ideas that have been established. Innovation is the development of a new idea that stands alone. It is imperative that creative abilities do not lie dormant and unused.

Complacency leads to the death of creativity. No matter how well a concept works, it should continually be reassessed with regard to creative improvement. *Success can be our greatest failure if it is not analyzed for improvement.*

> *". . . This is true of executives, leaders, and administrators in business and industry. They must be people who are capable of coping with the inevitable rapid obsolescence of any new product . . . We must define the skillful person or the trained person, or the educated person in a very different way than we used to (i.e., not as one who has a rich knowledge of the past so he can profit from past experiences in a future emergency). Much that we have learned has*

become useless. Any kind of learning, which is the simple application of the past to the present, or the use of past techniques in the present situation, has become obsolete in many areas of life. Education can no longer be considered essential or only a learning process; it is now also a character training, a person-training process . . . it will become truer and truer year by year . . . It means that we need people who are different from the average kind of person who confronts the present as if it were a repetition of the past, and who uses the present simply as a period in which he prepares for the future . . ."

Maslow, 1970

The more people "know" themselves, the more they will trust and have confidence in their abilities. People should not accept without questioning and assessing the ramifications of actions.

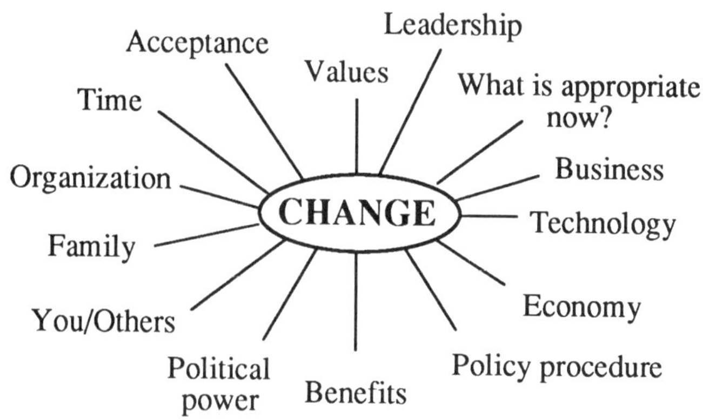

How quickly are these and other *stable* factors changing in your life?

CHANGE DEVELOPMENT

> *"Instead of developing an information base to be applied for the future, develop a self-process to manage change."*

> *"Learn to trust yourself in uncertain circumstances and separate yourself from the security of past events."*

> *"To improve, enhance, develop—change is inevitable!"*

Change—Adapting or developing alternatives for yourself and/or the environment. Here is an easy way to remember how you can make effective change:

C ourage to risk—to ask—to challenge—to meet future needs.

H ave an understanding of self/others and the situation.

A nalyze general to specific terms and concepts.

N eed to know—to research—to develop—to concur.

G o with your greatest strengths.

E xpected results should be identified.

Resistance to change lies in our perceived successes—because we have been successful, we do not want to change. This can be caused by a feeling of familiarity, safety, and security, or a feeling of "I can" that has been reinforced by tradition, standards, and competitors.

All new concepts eventually become outdated—continual improvement means change. Develop alternatives, adaptations, innovations, creativity, and problem solving to meet these future needs.

MOTIVATION AND CHANGE

Industrial psychologists have developed theories about organizations as they relate to employee behavior, and the role that employee motivation plays in that relationship. Motivation is a diffuse and complicated concept; it is influenced by many factors that vary from person to person and situation to situation. When we consider the array of scientific methods, management styles, and motivational studies, we must question how well these theories serve to define motivation in a way that is practically applicable.

An overview of motivation theories that lend themselves to the needs of industrial psychologists and executives and managers within organizations will be discussed. We'll examine two theories that began the modern understanding of motivating and leading employees: scientific method and the Hawthorne Study. In addition, other traditional motivation theories will be discussed and compared in terms of their applicability and usefulness in the workplace. Finally, we'll look at data collected on employees in terms of these motivation theories.

EARLY DEVELOPMENT OF MOTIVATION THEORIES

Some of the first systematic studies in industrial/organizational psychology were introduced by Frederick Taylor during the early 1900s (Taylor, 1911). Taylor is considered the father of scientific management in industrial engineering. His principle concepts included:

- Discover the best way to do a particular job.

- Divide the job into the simplest components.

- Establish piece (simple and repetitive) rate incentives.

Taylor's work led to studies that focused on workers' use of time and motion, and his work still strongly influences many new developments in workplace operations.

A recent documentary compared Soviet physicians' practice of removing cataracts (one that incorporates Taylor's ideas) with that of American surgeons. Ten Soviet physicians were seated while anesthetized patients, all prone on a conveyor belt, moved slowly in front of them. Each eye surgeon performed just one aspect of the cataract surgery. This practice meets Taylor's three criteria: the surgery is broken down into repetitive elements; each surgeon completes only one particular part of the surgery; and the patients are moved among the surgeons to have the completed procedure. Cataracts are a widespread problem among the Soviet population, and many people are on waiting lists for surgery. Thus, the demand for this operation is high, and because all medical care is provided by the state, the government clearly has an interest in keeping the costs necessary to eye surgery low. Possibly, Soviet surgeons adapted Taylor's theories, perhaps unknowingly, to their own practical business needs.

In addition to his piecework principles, Taylor made fundamental assumptions about workers that shaped the role they played in his work theories. He assumed that workers must be controlled and told what to do. Furthermore, Taylor's principle concepts began with three underlying assumptions about worker motivation:

1. Workers are motivated primarily by money (as we will discuss later, money is a lower form of motivation).

2. Workers are typically lazy and inefficient (which also suggests that workers are not achievement oriented).

3. Workers must be told what to do (which implies that workers are better followers than leaders).

Years later this concept would be labeled "Theory X" by Douglas McGregor, who adopted these concepts as a motivational management style (McGregor, 1960). A few years after Taylor's work, Mayo led several researchers to develop a very different and contrasting theory (Baron, 1986; Lawless, 1979).

In the Western Electric Hawthorne Plant, located in Chicago during the 1920s and 1930s, the researchers conducted a study that examined the effects of certain physical variables, such as levels of illumination and work breaks, with regard to employee behavior. As part of the research, they observed the workers in varying environments to see if productivity would change or improve. Quite aside from their original focus, Mayo and others found that the employees' consequent feelings of importance—because they were taking part in a study—caused improved productivity. Hereafter, this phenomenon was referred to as "The Hawthorne Effect."

The Hawthorne Effect claims that organizational change, regardless of its intent or content, produces a positive effect on worker motivation and performance (Statt, 1981). Basically, researchers concluded that informal group norms set standards and traditions within the organizational environment. Human relationships—among employees and between perceived management levels and employees—figure heavily in standard interactions between these groups. In other words, recognition of the worker is directly linked to worker productivity. This concept, which focuses on human relations in the workplace, correlates with what Douglas McGregor, years after the Hawthorne plant experiment, called Theory Y (McGregor, 1960). Theory Y essentially states that workers will generally perform a "good day's work" without overt direction from management.

Basically, the predictions resulting from the Hawthorne Study suggest that:

1. The average worker is motivated primarily by social factors.

2. Workers' attitudes are important to productivity, and they can be improved by providing a friendly work environment.

3. Satisfied workers generally are more productive.

Point 3 spawned an aphorism that appears throughout literature on this field: "Contented cows give more milk" (Baron, 1986; Lawless, 1979; Schein, 1980).

Over the years, however, the Hawthorne study has come under extensive review and, as will be discussed later, contentment or satisfaction may not necessarily correlate with productivity (Herzberg, 1966).

Workers have many needs, which may vary according to an individual's social-economic status, education, and goals. There is no one theory or psychological model that will encompass every problem or aspect of interaction in the workplace. All of these psychological concepts presented bring some insight— from various viewpoints—to the complex study of people in organizations.

MOTIVATION THEORY AND ITS ROLE IN THE WORKPLACE

The early organization studies by Taylor and Mayo served as the groundwork for much later theories about employee motivations.

Generally, motivation can be defined as the physical and mental effort expended toward a goal or standard (Baron, 1986; Lawless, 1979; Statt, 1981). Furthermore, motivation can be divided into two subcategories: extrinsic and intrinsic motivation (Harakiewecz, Abrahams, & Wageman, 1987). Extrinsic motivation is externally generated by recognition, praise, and rewards, such as a bonus or a promotion (Baron, 1986; Lawless, 1979). Taylor promoted extrinsic motivation; to elicit productivity from workers, he used control and payment.

Intrinsic motivation is internally generated; it might be described as achievement, pride in accomplishing, and a sense of fulfillment or self-actualization (Herzberg, 1966; Maslow, 1970). Concepts of internal motivation seem more closely aligned with The Hawthorne Effect; they depend on social aspects of the workplace and on the value of contentment and self-fulfillment to the employees.

Clearly, motivation is a casual factor in productivity and/or performance (Lawless, 1979; Baron, 1986). Many researchers use a basic formula to represent the relationship between productivity and performance and motivation:

Performance = Ability x Effort (or Motivation)

(Baron, 1986; Lawless, 1979; Schein, 1980; Statt, 1981.)

According to this formula, performance is the observed outcome of two variables, ability and motivation. Ability and motivation are indirectly observed and measured as they are demonstrated through employee performance.

For example, through observed performance a leader might accurately assess the level of effort, or the motivation of the employee. Keep in mind, however, that motivators are different for each employee; thus the question a leader must ask is, "What will cause this particular employee to become motivated?" The effect exerted on the job, correlated with the employee's ability (or competence), demonstrates the employee's level of performance.

We can further isolate motivation in order to identify if the employee is motivated as Taylor might imply, by the strict direction of a leader, or as Mayo might, by the social aspects or feelings of importance within the organization.

As we shall see from the several theoretical motivation models included here, there can be many causes for motivation. For instance, a commonly observed problem occurs when leaders attempt to motivate employees by focusing on their own motivational needs rather than those of the employees. As we delve further into the concept of motivation, this approach requires that the leader be other-directed—that is, recognize and respond to the employees' terms or levels as a basis for their motivation. The leader's perception of the employees' needs, as well as their perception of his/her managing style, are closely intertwined. According to Hall (1984), "Subordinates definitely bear and adopt as their own the manager's motivational message; managers create subordinates in their own image, and the image definitely differs as a function of the manager's level of achievement."

The challenge today's leader must meet, then, is that of motivating on the employees' level; if in fact external motivation is accepted by an employee, a leader must use it to maintain and/or enhance performance; if an employee values and responds to the social setting of his workplace, then the leader must consider ways to meet this need. As comparisons are made between each model, it is important to note that motivation is a complex issue in the workplace, particularly because each employee must be considered individually, and a leader can only assess these needs indirectly. It is also clear that this simple formula (Performance = Ability x Motivation) can only be used as a general representation—one that can be interpreted and applied in many different ways. In examining this model of motivation and performance and their uses, we will discuss the theories of McGregor, Maslow, Alderfer, McClelland, and Herzberg.

Both McGregor's Theory X and Theory Y management models make use of Taylor's and Mayo's concepts in different ways. Further investigation indicates that scientific management, and bureaucratic and hierarchical organizations, correlate to Theory X. Organizations with less bureaucracy and with more sharing of information and group interaction within the organizations adhere more closely to Theory Y (Baron, 1986; McGregor, 1960; Schein, 1980). Furthermore, McGregor indicated that leaders generally adopt a Theory X or Theory Y approach to motivate employees based on their own comfort level. Unfortunately, as noted earlier, most styles of management are based on individual styles rather than the comprehension level of employees and the situation (Hershey & Blanchard, 1976).

Again, keep in mind that according to Theory X, employees inherently do not like work and are lazy. According to Theory Y, employees experience working as a positive part of their lives, and given a structure that is responsive to their needs, they will seek challenge and responsibility. McGregor indicates that Theory Y is the most effective management style. However, the level of the employee in the organization and the work environment strongly influence the results of either management style. Both theories have merit according to the situation, time pressures, and/or the level of employee competence involved. When we consider both as general styles, Theory Y deals with the employee on a more humanistic basis and suggests a more flexible business approach (Hershey & Blanchard, 1976). Though Theory X has merit, we are more interested in exploring the possible applications of Theory Y.

This section contains data collected from large corporations listed in the top 100 American corporations (Gatto, 1985-1990). The results may support McGregor's Theory Y. The data was collected using Bernard Bass's Orientation Inventory, which measures three employee variables within the work environment:

a) *Self*—which reflects the extent to which people describe themselves as expecting direct rewards, regardless of the job they are doing, or the effect of what they do has upon others.

b) *Interaction*—which reflects the extent to which people are concerned with maintaining happy, harmonious relationships in a superficial way, which often makes it difficult to contribute to the task at hand or to be a real help to others.

c) *Task*—which reflects the extent to which people are concerned about completing a job, solving problems, working persistently, and doing the best job possible.

An employee who responds strongly to self, interaction, and task is an asset, but it is important to note here that the task that the employee may be motivated to perform may not coincide with what the leader or organization needs. Thus, we have examples of a situation in which Theory X, Y, or some combination of X and Y, might influence an employee's orientation greatly, depending on his/her level of competence and the required outcome.

The Orientation Inventory has 27 questions, and each question offers three alternative responses from which the participant can choose two: one that describes an individual's most-used action, then one describing a least-used action. The purpose of the Orientation Inventory is to diagnose individual style differences according to these three variables.

Data from the study yielded the following results.

	N - 1046	
Self	194	19%
Interaction	109	10%
Task	743	71%

Based on these data, the application of the theories suggested by the Hawthorne studies and McGregor's Theory Y concept is a valid approach. The Hawthorne Effect and Theory Y concept indicate that employees are concerned with working, performing and getting the job done, and having a positive work experience, given the availability of appropriate working conditions. In other words, these results indicate that employees are primarily task oriented rather than self- or interaction oriented. Assuming these finds as a basis, management's next step is to find the most appropriate ways to motivate task-oriented employees, and then to create an environment that will offer opportunities to stimulate this task orientation.

The self- and interaction-oriented employees might benefit the organization best (through productivity) if the Theory X approach is used. If these individuals are asked to respond to the same motivation as task-oriented employees, they might be perceived as indolent because they will not focus on their task; they may wander from—or refuse to fulfill—the desired outcome within the time frame.

Again, these data indicate that employees are not lazy and that they do not require a high level of management control, as argued by Taylor and other Theory X proponents; instead they are in need of an opportunity to develop self-growth through task achievement. This is not to suggest that an employee requires no other impetus to accept a leader's work agenda; as McGregor points out, Theory Y is a better approach to motivating employees. Theory Y also allows a leader to add extrinsic motivation—in the form of praising employees and helping them to succeed at their jobs—which leads again to the intrinsic motivation of self-fulfillment. The primary consideration in creating this system is identifying what precedes task orientation and what will appropriately motivate employees to focus on the performance of needed tasks.

As a resource for developing these motivation methods and a complementary environment, consider some additional psychological motivational models. For instance, Maslow's Need Hierarchy postulates five needs that are hierarchical and common to all people: an individual's physiological needs are the most basic and primary concern, then safety or security, a sense of "belongingness," social esteem, and, finally, self-actualization (Maslow, 1970).

Alderfer developed a model very similar to Maslow's, but his model has only three variables: Existence (E), which is similar to Maslow's physiological/safety; Relatedness (R), similar to "belongingness"; and Growth (G), which is similar to self-esteem and self-actualization. Often this composite is referred to as ERG. The ERG concept suggests that unmet needs result in a "frustration-regression" pattern, which can produce an increased concern or desire for a lower-level need. As an example, consider workers who are well paid, but because their jobs are boring, they want more money. The frustration of not having a challenging job is somewhat compensated by money.

Both Maslow's and Alderfer's models are easily applied to the workplace. For instance, Porter (1975) found that leaders rate growth, esteem, and self-actualization as most important among employees, but that self-actualization needs appeared to be continually sought by leaders; in other words, there is an insatiable need to fully achieve one's potential.

The concept of task orientation is comparable to these two psychological models. The desire and ability to get a job accomplished may, at times, be cause for frustration if the task is not challenging, or if an employee perceives an opportunity for achievement as negligible.

The challenge a job offers certainly correlates with the commitment an employee can invest in the job, but this commitment might require the added strength or attraction that money offers. Most employees respond to money because it represents a trade-off for recognition and success within the workplace (Baron, 1986; Lawless, 1979). Often a competitive salary or wage translates as success and recognition, which might manifest itself as purchase of a car, house, clothes, or as the community in which a person lives.

This combination of extrinsic (praise and/or money) and intrinsic (challenge and/or self-fulfillment) motivators leads to another helpful model, McClelland's concept of motivation. McClelland suggested that motivation could be understood through three concepts: achievement, power, and affiliation.

Ideally, an individual pursues achievement through the challenge of reaching a goal or successfully completing a task. In contrast, low achievers complete a task to avoid failure or punishment. This polarity is reminiscent of an old argument: Is the individual person inherently good or evil? One can argue that people are good, and therefore, we create systems and write laws that benefit us. On the other hand, one might argue that people are fundamentally evil, that we must create systems and write laws that punish, so that evil people will obey the law and act correctly out of fear (Eitzen, 1978). This argument correlates to the task-oriented worker who is internally motivated and to the indolent worker, whom the leader must constantly work to control.

Inherent in this argument is a twofold understanding of power. An individual is motivated to fulfill needs through personal power, which involves having authority over others, having the capability to make others follow one's orders, or through social power, which dominates others, but disperses this domination in a socially acceptable manner. Social power is authority applied to a particular situation; it is power focused on a constructive outcome. "Power [is] the basic energy to initiate and sustain action, translating intention into reality, the quality without which leaders cannot lead" (Bennis & Nanus, 1988). Power is the motivation that causes leaders to succeed in achieving a vision while giving followers a direction to embrace.

Maslow's model, like McClelland's, assumes that power is an inherent part of motivation, and McClelland's affiliation need is similar to what Maslow identifies as the need to belong to a group. People focused on this need level are motivated primarily to form and maintain interpersonal relationships while avoiding conflicts.

McClelland's motivational model has been tested through the use of diagnostic pictures. By having clients describe what they see in a picture, the psychologist better understands their motivating factors.

A correlation exists between such motivation profiles (like Theories X and Y) and leaders who are high, average, or low achievers. When the two models are correlated, a new dimension emerges as a method of analyzing the motivational level of leaders and employees.

> *"The motivational assumptions of Low Achieving managers correspond in significant ways to the pessimistic, reductive view of the working man, which Douglas McGregor dubbed Theory X. High Achiever perspectives, on the other hand, are consistent with the more positive developmental beliefs embodied in McGregor's Theory Y. Average Achievers fall somewhere in between pure Theory X and Theory Y . . . essentially Theory X tempered with human relations training or related experience."*

Hall, 1984

Thus, it seems clear that one's self-perception is a very powerful self-motivator, and that it acts as a catalyst to forming one's leadership style, especially in terms of motivating employees.

Finally, with this focus on the self and a leader's self-perception, we come to Herzberg's theory. McClelland's three concepts—achievement, power, and affiliation—correlate somewhat to Herzberg's hygienes: satisfiers, which are intrinsic motivators such as achievement, advancement, and the challenge of the job, and dissatisfiers, which are extrinsic motivators such as salary, benefits, and company policies. These two interrelated concepts, satisfiers (motivators) and dissatisfiers (hygienes), generally correlate with our earlier designations of intrinsic and extrinsic motivation.

Each of these psychological motivational models and theories can be used to describe and analyze employee-management interaction in a work setting. They lend themselves to the field of industrial counseling in a way that many psychological theories do not. This concept of motivation is not easy to describe and apply, particularly in terms of employees as a group, rather than as individuals. Motivation is illusive and dynamic, and it is shaped by rapport, tradition, and standards. An effective and useful conceptualization of motivation is one that allows us to examine, in a very real sense, the needs and levels of employees in a particular workplace. We must account for the needs and motivations of the company itself, and yet, on an individual basis, guide people toward self-development.

Comparing Herzberg's model with Maslow's further indicates the difference between hygiene and motivators. One major difference that must be pointed out is that Maslow's theoretical model is built on a hierarchy, while Herzberg's model has no such precondition.

<table>
<tr><td align="center">MASLOW</td><td align="center">HERZBERG</td></tr>
</table>

MASLOW	HERZBERG
Self-actualization	**Motivator Factors**
creativity	**(Satisfiers)**
self-realization	achievement
challenges of work	advancement
	opportunity
Self-esteem	appreciation
promotion, praise	praise
special benefits	earned recognition
belonging	personal growth
teamwork, social groups	acceptance
friendly manager	work itself
Safety	**Hygiene Factors**
job security	**(Dissatisfiers)**
work standards	wages
seniority	work conditions
Psychological	company policies
money	organizational structure
work breaks	co-workers
equipment	management personalities
work conditions	facilities

(Herzberg, Maslow, Hall)

The point is that Herzberg's dissatisfiers offer motivation aimed at Maslow's lower needs, while the satisfiers offer motivation aimed at higher needs. The better the leader and employee can combine the employee's intrinsic motivation with the external motivation provided and demonstrated by the leader, the better the performance level of the employee. In other words, identify a cause for motivation and provide that level of motivation. Of course, an obvious problem arises when a high achieving leader—one who responds best to Theory Y and bases a leadership style on Theory Y—perceives that motivation is best sowed through Herzberg's motivating factors when employees are focused on hygiene motivators. The problem within motivation now truly emerges as complex and illusive.

SUMMARY

We've presented a brief historical perspective on some models and theories of motivation that particularly lend themselves to the needs of workplace psychology and industrial counselors. In comparing, analyzing, and examining each theory, including Scientific Management and the Hawthorne Effect, and in finding correlations between McGregor's work and the results of the author's research, we can say that no single theory describes leadership style or fulfills the management needs of any company. Maslow's, Alderfer's, McClelland's, and Herzberg's theories are all necessary. In shaping a leadership style, however, you must identify the concerns and needs of the employees as well as your own and those of the organization. In addition, you must consider which model of motivation you are comfortable with, both in terms of practical application and of your own perception of people and the situation.

Motivation is easily discussed, but it is successfully incorporated as an element of management style only through rapport, trust, and consistent follow-up between the leader, employees, and the organization. It is this diffuse and complicated concept that changes from person to person, that causes organizations to be successful and to strive to achieve the concept of organizational quality.

9

A SHARING OF YOURSELF

To succeed at anything, you have to have a concept of self—a feeling of what you can do, who you are. You also need this concept of "self" reinforced by others. This gives a sense of reality to your internal concept. There needs to be a balance between how you know yourself, your core capacity, and your abilities in conjunction with the external concepts or reinforcement from others.

Often there is a self-understanding (introspection) and an awareness of how others view you (interpersonal feedback). There also is a separate concept of true reality—a gray concept—between the clearer concepts (black and white) of self and others' views.

An analogy would be the tragic figure of Wolfgang Mozart. Mozart felt and knew he was a genius. During his life, he was known as a fine musician, but lacking in certain abilities musically and socially. After his death, he was recognized as a genius.

Success is knowing and understanding your capacity of self and having that reinforced by others. This concept of self, and evaluation of self, creates a sense of how to become your potential. The question is, have we challenged ourselves in the proper manner to sufficiently stimulate our core capacity of realizing our potential?

Because of external reinforcement, or the lack thereof, human potential is continually directed, focused, redirected, and refocused. We are flexible people continually evolving and changing. Change is the ability to know and understand our own needs and flexibilities that should be redirected and/or refocused. Our concept of self-involvement and reactions in a particular environment are most important. Resistance to change is the security and safety found in the original application and/or focus of thought and our own unwillingness to accept new self-understanding, redirection, and/or refocused application.

Internal conflict arises when the self-understanding and reinforcement from others are not balanced and equal. You could have wants and needs that are not supported or even desired by others. This, then, creates an internal conflict of what to do.

How can you become your potential? How can we influence others to accept us as we accept ourselves or vice versa: How can we accept ourselves as others see us?

IT DOESN'T TAKE A GENIUS

All human beings have a capacity to become what is classified as genius. Two concepts hold us back from finding that genius: (1) it is never defined by ourselves or others; (2) it is not accepted by ourselves and others as genius.

An example of the first concept might be that many people could have been concert pianists or artists, but never took a music or art lesson in their life. The second example would be that the musical or artistic genius was identified through music and art lessons, but not accepted (valued) as a focus or direction by ourselves or by others (instructors, etc.) who influenced the concept of self (who we are).

The concept of self as human beings striving to find meaning is an important one. We need to have a balance of who we are—defining our genius—through an internal and external concept. We all possess the potential to be a genius—but a genius at what?

It is important to think of life as a processing toward self-accomplishment and/or fulfillment of our core capacity. This will help to lead into a direction of flexibility and adapting to situational concepts of becoming fully human. This is an important element of leadership as well as living a fulfilling life.

What is acceptable in one changing environment (home life) might not be acceptable or appropriate in another changing environment (work or student life). The better we know ourselves, the better we will be able to compare others to ourselves. This creates a rationalization of acceptance for ourselves within a particular changing environment. We must be able to balance the concept of what is appropriate in a given circumstance, understanding internal (self-concept) and the external (others' concepts) actions that reinforce our behavior.

As a leader, the concepts of appropriate and inappropriate are not opposite concepts. If an action is appropriate, it is accepted. If it is not accepted it lacks being appropriate for now, given a particular environment (people, equipment, logistics). If something is inappropriate, that is to say that you and/or others do not accept the actions or thoughts given a certain environment, it might be appropriate in the future. The concept of appropriate/inappropriate is continually being redefined through the laws, corporate policy, religious doctrine, societal norms, etc.

Leaders should view external influences (others, environment) in relationship to the self-concepts of understanding. Self-expectations and acceptance (i.e., self-love) are concepts that should be influenced, but not compromised to the point of sacrificing the core capacity or potential that dwells inside of self.

Leaders need to have a sense of self and honor those concepts, as well as have an understanding and honoring of external reinforcement. Perceived reality should be an understanding of our core capacity being influenced. The concept of becoming is an eclectic defining of our core capacity potential (internal and external influence) within a changing environment (technology, truth, understanding).

Leaders need to strive to define meaning for ourselves to define the concept of self and knowing others. Unfortunately, too often the concept of self is not honored, rather, self is defined by the external influence. This begins at birth, through family influence, formal education, and the work environment. Self needs to surface as the honoring of self-understanding and the meaning and justification of striving to fulfill the core capacity—potentials (kernels) waiting to be nurtured to develop to create the beautiful emergence of oneself. Within that development of self should be an autonomous self-assurance and reliance.

Meaning and development of self should not be a symbiotic relationship or adoption of another's concept of self (me). The self (internal) concept should create meaning by nurturing one's core capacity (potential, talents) that is supported and/or accepted by others' (external) concepts. The balance of striving to become within a given and/or changing environment is not an arrival. It is a constant striving to become.

BUILDING SELF-ESTEEM

The concept of learning in early childhood and grade school should be the development of self-worth and confidence that emerges into *"I am."*

The "I am" concept is a nurturing of the emotional and intellectual core capacity of innate abilities within the existence of particular, evolving, and changing environments. Before we acquire knowledge that defines a particular way of life, it is paramount to define self-trust in uncertain circumstances. We need to know that we can change self and environmental needs.

Each human exists in an environment of experiences to which they have to mentally adapt. There are two influences in any circumstance: (1) the innate mental ability to know and apply, and (2) the environment that is provided. We should know and analyze an environment and realize our interactive abilities within that environment. Although one might be excellent working within a particular environment, it does not ensure that the person can function well in another environment or interaction.

Today, leaders must feel secure with the circumstances whether or not they can meet self-imposed expectations. Self-esteem and self-trust help you function in unclear circumstances. Knowing yourself means that imposed expectations are exposed rationally, logically, intuitively, creatively, and emotionally.

Unfortunately, when you find yourself in an uncertain situation, the influencing mental function is an emotional, *"I like or dislike"* concept, which creates meaning. Another reaction is, *"I can function,"* which is trusting yourself even when you're not an expert about a job responsibility. We can have confidence in ourselves separate from job esteem.

For example, a leader might be an emotionally revealing and inspiring speaker, yet not able to use a word processor. Because the leader cannot use a word processor does not mean that the leader is a failure. He/She still should have a sense of esteem that functions even knowing of an inability to function in uncertain environments or circumstances. However, the observation made by many is that employees fall into the lowest level within the circumstance rather than knowing their self-concept (I am) well enough to compare "I can" and "cannots" in a rationale sense.

The balance of self-discovery and the influence of others is a diligent mental function. We all want to be accepted, have a sense of belonging, be intimate, know and share experiences with others. We need to have a sense of value that creates meaning. We need to seek what satisfies and creates meaning for our life.

The satisfaction of need and the creation of meaning are formulated, shaped, and developed through a process of making choices. The choices we make strengthen and mold the concept of "I am." The choices of job, spouse, educational direction, and environment interaction are all dependent on the confidence of self. As leaders, the interaction between what is available and how we utilize it creates an influencing concept perceived by others. They watch, compare, and subjectively interpret (creating meaning for themselves) the exposed behavior (I am).

Through interactive expression we can greatly influence others' perception as well as develop a self-concept. Leaders can create alternatives, problem solve, and gain satisfaction by generating and nurturing the value system, philosophy, and confidence to achieve potentials. Through utilizing available choices, given an environment and interacting with others, our core capacity to become is nurtured.

The more leaders challenge and question, the more we can strengthen our understanding of who "I am." Like a weight lifter pushing the muscle to a point of exhaustion, so should we push the mental capacity to logical and creative exhaustion. As the environment, societal needs, and self-needs change, so will the mental wherewithal leaders need to meet the new environment. Developing mental wherewithal is important to developing potential abilities—for self and others.

RECOGNIZING SUCCESS

Success is not an achievement, accolade, or award. Success is not the winner of an event. Success is not how much money you make. Success is the introspective understanding of fulfillment. A fulfillment through the utilization of innate abilities. It is a self-understanding—a self-appreciation—of an emotional and logical self-gratification. You feel successful when success is identified and present in your mind. Success is the realization that you have achieved an expectation, that moment in which sadness is absent and an overwhelming self-fulfillment that is interpreted as "I can" and "I did" parallel. Success cannot be defined by someone else—someone else cannot dictate another's expectations. Yet, most people dwell on what they *didn't* do. How many business meetings have you attended in order to better understand and discuss success versus going to a meeting to discuss a problem or failure?

It is important for leaders to identify a particular aspect of self—self-understanding in which we credit ourselves. The statement, *"You are too hard on yourself,"* is a statement that might lack self-love and understanding in realistic terms. We can be successful every moment; unfortunately, we take ourselves for granted and judge ourselves not to be worthy of success because of lack of an all-knowing ability to compare any external influences.

Success—although expressed to others—is an internal understanding. The better we understand the "I am" concept, the better we will understand that we have achieved and are successful. External parameters of job, salary, and perks are not indications of success. Unfortunately, many people vicariously equate these external forces to be success and never clearly define a concept of needed accomplishment for themselves. Success is a feeling of inner peace, job satisfaction, and acceptance of who you are. Some external parameters are only signs of success. Successful people create for themselves an acceptance of "me." *Although in my life "I" have done inappropriate acts given the environment or circumstance, I still have an understanding of who I am and my ability to be successful in other environments. They continue to challenge—look ahead and address difficulty.*

To create meaning of any concept, we should contemplate and reflect on possibilities, in relationship to growth potential. The more we explore our relationships and alternatives/actions, the more we will expand our understanding of ourselves and be able to give credit for our successes.

Failure, like success, is not universal—it is an internal experience of denial of the humanness of trying. Success *and* failure can be catalysts for mental growth, although failure is often a better learning experience than success. We rationalize and analyze our failures and ask, *"What went wrong?"*

To succeed as a leader, we must analyze self, ask questions, and create an understanding and acceptance of ourselves. We have the freedom to choose, and should accept ourselves unconditionally. That is not to say we should deem every act as being appropriate given the circumstance. There should be acts of behavior that embarrass, challenge, and frustrate, as well as exhilarate. To know and understand what we value, what we are willing to fight for, and what we want to achieve.

Success is the feeling and understanding of self-acceptance that we should strive to become. We all have a potential to choose, know, experience, and succeed. The more we accept ourselves, the more we will become through that acceptance.

"Leaders need to: be competent and confident,
initiate appropriate action, clearly communicate,
actively listen to others, know their followers,
and be flexible and willing to lead."

DEFINITIONS

Business Meeting

Coming together to fulfill certain business expectations; sharing, collecting, and disseminating information with all in attendance; establishing responsibilities for attending members and establishing an agenda for follow-up actions within a specific time frame.

Decision-making Process

There are several types of decision-making processes. Consider the type of problem, time, and the needed results or outcomes.

Unilateral—One person makes a decision alone—time might be a factor.

Consensus Decision—The general commitment by the members of a group in which all are involved, all points of view are discussed, and all input is assessed—usually the most effective and creative decision.

Majority Decision—Agreement of group members by more than half of the group—democracy.

Strong Minority Decision—Cliques that support or influence each other and may even create a split in the group decision—small but vocal group; might dominate.

Unanimous Decision—All of the members of the group are in total agreement.

Effective Communication/Presentation

Establishing a mutual understanding or comprehension about particular information, given the presenter's abilities and skills and the listener's abilities to comprehend within a specific environment.

Effective Listening

Receiving verbal information, interpreting it, developing a concept of what is said, and not being overly influenced by how it is said or who said it; clarifying what is said in order to establish a mutual understanding of what follow-up action—mentally and behaviorally—is expected within a changing environment.

Employee

One who fulfills management's concepts, supervisory expectations, corporate policy, and customer/client needs (follower).

Expected Results

That which one wants to accomplish; the adoption of business concepts that are expected to be fulfilled within a specific time frame; established goals; a focused working direction.

Influencer

Those who gain support and have others comply with their thoughts whether they do or do not have the formal authority to have others comply.

Measurable Actions

Methods, strategies, and behaviors that utilize acquired knowledge to accomplish expected results; the application of acquired knowledge that eventually leads to the fulfillment of expected results (established objectives).

Responsibility

That which one is willing to accept given one's abilities in a changing environment. Accountability, pride, acceptance.

Setting Priorities

Establish priorities, then utilize periods of time to meet necessary priorities. This is accomplished by using problem solving—developing alternatives—given the changing environment, available resources, and motivation of you and others to focus energies on the same necessary priorities.

Skills

Utilizing one's abilities to apply acquired information—knowledge, awareness—over periods of time—relaxed, stressful. The adaptation of one's abilities within changing environments to meet perceived needs. Skill is the perceived observation of ability.

Team Building

The process of individuals coming together to share energies (synergism) in an open, honest, trusting, and respectful manner to address and achieve business-related concepts by creating and molding a unified plan of action.

REFERENCES

Argyris, C. (1973). <u>Intervention theory and method—a behavioral science view</u>. Massachusetts: Addison-Wesley Publishing Co.

Alderfer, C. (1972). <u>Existence, relatedness and growth</u>. New York: Free Press.

Baron, R. (1986). <u>Behavior in organization</u> (2nd ed.). Boston: Allyn and Bacon.

Bass, B. (1985). <u>Leadership and performance beyond expectations</u>. New York: MacMillan Publishing Co.

Bass, B. (1987). <u>Manual for the orientation inventory</u>. Palo Alto, CA: Consulting Psychologists Press.

Bass, B. (1981). <u>Stogdill's handbook of leadership</u>. New York: MacMillan Publishing Co.

Bennis, W., & Nanus, B. (1985). <u>Leaders—the strategies for taking charge</u>. New York: Harper and Row.

Bennis, W. (1989). <u>Why leaders can't lead</u>. Training and Development Journal, page 36.

Bion, W. R. (1959). <u>Experiences in groups</u>. New York: Basics Books.

Charrier, G. (1974). <u>Cog's ladder: a model of group development</u>. The 1974 Annual Handbook for Group Facilitators, University Associates. La Jolla, CA, pages 142-145.

Depree, M. (1989). <u>Leadership is an art</u>. New York: Dell Publishing Group, Inc.

Drucker, P. (1964). <u>Managing for results</u>. New York: Harper and Row.

Drucker, P. (1954). <u>The practice of management</u>. New York: Harper and Row.

Dunnette, M. (1976). (Ed.) <u>Handbook of industrial and organizational psychology</u>. Chicago: Rand-McNally.

Egan, G. (1986). <u>The skilled helper: A systematic approach to effective helping</u>. Belmont, CA: Brooks/Cole.

Eitzen, S. (1976). <u>In conflict and order: Understanding society</u>. Boston: Ally and Bacon.

FYI Video (1990). <u>Bring out the leader in you</u>. [Video]. Saranac Lake, NY: AMA Public Service.

Golembiewski, R.T. (1962). <u>The small group</u>. Chicago: University of Chicago Press.

Hall, J. (1984). <u>Closing the loop</u>. Woodlands, TX: Woodstead Press.

Hall, J. (1988). <u>Models of management: The structure of competence</u>. Woodlands, TX: Woodstead Press.

Harackiewicz, J., Abrahams, A., & Wageman, R. (1987). Performance evaluation and intrinsic motivation: The effects of evaluative focus, rewards and achievement orientation. <u>Journal of Personality and Social Psychology</u>. 53, 1014-1023.

Harvey, J.B. (1974). The Abilene Paradox: The Management of Agreement. <u>Organizational Dynamics</u>, Summer.

Hawking, S. (1988). <u>A brief history of time</u>. New York: Prentice-Hall.

Hershey, P., & Blanchard, K. (1976). <u>Situational leadership</u>. San Diego: Center for Leadership Studies.

Herzberg, F. (1966). <u>One more time: How do you motivate employees?</u> <u>Harvard Business Review</u>, September, Pages 1-10.

Herzberg, F. (1966). <u>Work and nature of man</u>. Cleveland: World Publishing.

Juran, J. (1989). <u>Juran on leadership for quality</u>. New York: MacMillan.

Karp, H.B. (1985). <u>Personal power: An unorthodox guide to success</u>. New York: American Management Association.

Knowles, M. & Knowles, H. (1972). <u>Introduction to group dynamics</u>. Englewood Cliffs, NJ: Prentice-Hall.

Lawless, D. (1979). <u>Organizational behavior</u> (2nd ed.). Englewood Cliffs, NJ: Prentice-Hall.

Learn from the best (1990, May). <u>Quality Progress</u>.

Lewin, K. Field (1951). <u>Theory in social science</u>, Darwin Cartwright Ed. New York: Harper & Brothers, p. 169.

Luft, J. <u>Group processes: An introduction to group dynamics</u> (3rd ed.). San Francisco: Mayfield Publishing.

Maslow, A. (1970). <u>Motivation on personality</u> (2nd ed.). New York: Harper and Row.

Mayo, E. (1933). <u>The human problems of an industrial civilization</u>. New York: Macmillan.

McClelland, D.C. (1962, July/August). Business drive and national achievement. <u>Harvard Business Review,</u> pp. 99-112.

McClelland, D.C. (1965, November/December). Achievement motivation can be developed. <u>Harvard Business Review</u>, pp. 64-70.

McGregor, D. (1960). <u>The human side of enterprise</u>. New York: McGraw-Hill.

Osborn, A.F. (1963). <u>Applied imagination</u> (3rd rev. ed.). New York: Scribners.

Ouchi, W.G. (1981). <u>Theory 2: How American business can meet the Japanese challenge</u>. Massachusetts: Addison-Wesley Publishing Co.

Peters, T. & Waterman, R. Jr. (1982). <u>In search of excellence</u>. New York: Harper and Row.

Peters, T. (1987). <u>Thriving on chaos</u>. New York: Alfred A. Knopf.

Porter, L., Lawler, E., & Hachman, R. (1975). <u>Behavior in organization</u>. New York: McGraw-Hill.

Schein, E. H. (1980). <u>Organization psychology</u> (3rd ed.). Englewood Cliffs, NJ: Prentice-Hall.

Statt, D. (1981). <u>Dictionary of psychology</u>. New York: Harper and Row.

Tuckman, B. W. (1965). Developmental Sequences in Small Groups. <u>Psychological Bulletin</u> 63, pp. 384-399.

Tobias, L. (1990). <u>Psychological consulting to management: A clinician's perspective</u>. New York: Brunner/Mazel.

Yeomans, W. (1985). <u>1000 Things you never learned in business school</u>. New York: McGraw-Hill.

Dr. Gatto is also the author of <u>A Practical Guide to Effective Presentation</u>, considered to be *the* handbook for effective one-on-one or group communication.

He has also recently published <u>Controlling Stress in the Workplace</u>, a businessperson's one-stop handbook for reducing stress.

To order other publications
or for more information, call:

1 800 742-5482